MW00471156

BREW CLASSIC EUROPEAN BEERS AT HOME

Graham
Wheeler
and
Roger
Protz

BOOKS

Authors: Graham Wheeler
and Roger Protz

Design: Rob Howells
Cover artwork: Roger Gorringe

Typeset by T&O Graphics, Broome,
Bungay, Suffolk
Printed by WSOY, Finland

ISBN 1 85249 117 5

Published by CAMRA Books, Campaign
for Real Ale Ltd, 230 Hatfield Road,
St Albans AL1 4LW

© CAMRA Books 1995

First published December 1995

Conditions of sale:
This book shall not, by way of trade or
otherwise, be lent, resold, hired out or
otherwise circulated without the publish-
er's prior consent in any form of binding
or cover other than in which it is published and without similar conditions
being imposed on the subsequent pur-
chaser. This book is published at a net
price and supplied subject to the
Publishers Association Standard
Conditions of Sale registered under the
Restrictive Trade Practices Act 1956. All
rights reserved. No parts of this publica-
tion may be reproduced, stored in
retrieval systems, or transmitted in any
form or by any means, electronic,
mechanical, photocopying or otherwise,
without the prior permission of CAMRA
Books.

Contents

Introduction

Graham Wheeler and I have the perfect working relationship. He brews superb beer. I drink it. Graham, with the aid of recipes, a computer and his own mini brewery in his garden shed, has recreated classic ales and lagers from the British Isles and mainland Europe. My role has been more than that of a taster. The beers chosen for this book are the result of my own researches and travels over many years and the wheedling of recipes from often reluctant brewers.

The aim of the book is a simple one: to present to dedicated home-brewers recipes that will enable you to recreate some of the finest beers in the world. Beer is emerging from the long shadow cast by wine and wine-snobbery. Beer has heritage and history. Ale brewing goes back 3,000 years BC. Commercial lager brewing is a child of the industrial revolution though primitive lagering or cold conditioning of beer is much older.

Both styles offer a profusion of aromas and flavours, richly malty, tartly and bitterly hoppy plus, in the case of ales and stronger lagers, fascinating and delicious fruitiness created by fermentation. In a world of increasing conformity, craft brewers in Europe and the United States are now reproducing genuine India Pale Ales, porters, stouts, Pilsners, Budweisers, Alts, Kölsch, Bocks and many more. Now we offer home-brewers the exciting ability to make these great beer styles in your own homes.

Good brewing and good drinking. See you in the garden shed.
Roger Protz

About this book

GRAHAM WHEELER

Welcome to another collection of recipes for the home brewing enthusiast. This compendium of recipes emulates well-known beers from mainland Europe, although a few British styles that were not included in my previous efforts have been thrown in for good measure. There are recipes for Belgian ales, dark lagers, Pilsners, Alts, smoked beers, wheat beers, spiced beers, soured beers, Märzens, bocks, sweet stouts and bières de garde; in fact every style of beer that we could get sufficient information about to enable us to design a suitable recipe.

Again I have used well-known commercial brand names as a good way of communicating a particular style or flavour of beer, but I must stress that it is quite unlikely that any particular recipe herein will be an exact duplicate of the commercial brewer's beer. The recipes have, in fact, been based upon information supplied by the brewers, but that information was often incomplete. In some cases it has been necessary to take some blind guesses, but I hope that the combined knowledge and experience of Roger and myself will mean that those guesses are fairly accurate. Language barriers make a book like this particularly difficult to write. It is not easy to pick up the phone and ask a head brewer somewhere in Europe what he actually means by certain statements that do not translate well. Similar ingredients are often given different names in different countries and because of the very wide range of ingredients used throughout Europe, far too many to realistically expect the home-brew trade to stock, it has sometimes been necessary to reformulate recipes to use ingredients that are more readily available. In many cases the home-brewed beer will match the commercial prototype head on, but the recipes should be taken as accurately reflecting the beer-style rather than being a duplicate of the commercial beer.

My previous books were written for the British home brewing hobby, but nevertheless they have found their way into America, Australia, Canada, Japan, New Zealand, Scandinavia and Europe. Therefore, with a world-wide market in mind, this book is rather more world-friendly than my previous efforts. It is multimetric I suppose; each recipe has four variations with quantities given for batches of 25 litres, 23 litres, 5 UK gals and 5 US gals. The gallon volumes have the ingredients specified in pounds and ounces and the litre volumes in grams. Gravities are given in both specific gravity and degrees Plato; temperatures in Centigrade (Celsius) and Fahrenheit; alcohol by weight and volume and so on. Malt extract versions of some beers are given for those who prefer to brew that way.

This book is not really for the beginner. There simply is not enough space to enter into discussions on basic brewing theory or detailed descriptions of brewing technique. For that reason there is little in the way of theory contained within these pages. What I have done is to provide general indications of the brewing method that I consider appropriate for each beer and brief instructions on how to achieve it in a fairly matter-of-fact manner and I have assumed that the reader has enough knowledge to know what I am talking about. Where an unusual technique has particular relevance to the beer in question I have elaborated on the subject, but this is not a comprehensive brewing manual; there is little point in wasting space on reiterating familiar material. There is an increasing number of good books covering basic home brewing methods and theory, most enthusiastic brewers have several on their shelves, thus the reader is directed to one of those if he or she requires more general information.

Wassail

Graham Wheeler

Fermentable Ingredients

MALTED BARLEY

The basis of all beer is barley, malted barley to be precise, usually referred to simply as malt. Malted barley is barley that has been soaked in water and allowed to germinate. When germination has proceeded far enough it is halted by drying the malt. It is baked in a kiln to ensure that it is dried properly and roasted to the desired colour. During the malting process, the hard, impervious kernel of the grain is converted into a friable, biscuity material that can be readily crushed and wetted with water.

The conversion process during malting is known as modification. An under-modified malt is one where germination has not been allowed to proceed far enough, leaving part of the grain unconverted, resulting in an inefficient malt. Part of the corn, usually one end, remains "hard". An over-modified malt will also produce an inefficient malt, because if germination is allowed to proceed past its optimum the extended respiration of the barley continues to use up starch reserves that we need during mashing. A well-modified malt is one where the maltster (or the programmer who wrote the software) judged it just right, and the whole corn has been converted without excessive wastage of substrate.

Malted barley contains two major components that are important to the brewer and these must be present in a certain ratio to each other and within certain limits for the malt to be regarded as good for brewing purposes. The first of these is starch. Starch is a complex carbohydrate which is converted into simpler forms during malting, then converted to a range of sugars during mashing, and ultimately converted to alcohol and body during fermentation. Without this starch there would not be beer, and the more of it there is, the greater is the efficiency of the malt. In other words the greater will be the fermentable extract achieved from the malt.

The second of these important components is protein. Protein is not a single substance but a group of complex nitrogenous substances. During malting high-level proteins and other nitrogenous substances contained in the outer layer of the grain are converted into simpler proteins, soluble proteins, amino-acids, peptides, and enzymes; all of which can be regarded as nitrogenous components.

Unfortunately, protein levels can be a thorn in the brewer's side.

4

Some nitrogen cum protein is necessary because we need the action of enzymes during malting and mashing, and we need amino-acids and other nitrogenous components as food for the yeast during fermentation, but if we have too much protein then problems begin to show themselves. One problem is that nitrogen and starch are mutually exclusive: the higher the nitrogen cum protein content of the malt, the less starch there will be, and the poorer will be the fermentable material extracted from the malt.

By far the biggest problem, however, is that malt with too much protein will cause a hazy beer. A protein haze is both tasteless and harmless, but it will certainly spoil the appearance of the beer somewhat. To a commercial brewer a hazy pale ale would be unsaleable, although it would taste fine from a pewter tankard.

A protein haze manifests itself in two basic forms: permanent haze and chill haze. Permanent haze, as its name suggests, is a protein haze that is always present. It is caused by semi-soluble proteins that come out of solution but, nevertheless, still remain in suspension. A chill haze is a similar haze that manifests itself when the beer is chilled, but which usually disappears when the beer is warmed up again. This happens because the solubility of some proteins decreases with temperature. The effect of chill haze can be quite dramatic; I have seen a beer change from golden clarity to dark, murky, opacity with a temperature change of only about 4°C below room temperature.

Unfortunately, both forms of haze get worse with age. A protein haze usually gradually builds up with time. During a beer's lifetime, complex reactions are continually taking place between proteins, tannins, and other components in the beer, producing protein complexes that become less and less soluble. A beer that was crystal-clear and well-behaved when bottled could be hazy or even opaque a few weeks later. If the protein is really excessive the beer could haze from the moment it is brewed, and the problem is greatest, of course, with beers that are expected to be highly chilled, such as lager.

The best way of preventing such problems is to ensure that the malt has a minimal level of protein in the first place. It therefore follows that the best-quality brewing malts are those that are relatively low in nitrogen. Nitrogen content and protein content are linked and both are used by brewers to indicate very much the same thing; the brewing value of the malt. Nitrogen and protein are deemed to be present in the ratio of approximately 1:6.25, thus if one is known the approximate value of the other can be found. A malt with 1.5 per cent total nitrogen will contain about 9.4 per cent protein.

Low nitrogen malt is essential for the traditional, British, infusion mash brewing method, but low-nitrogen barley is difficult to grow and goes against modern commercial sensibilities. The types of barley that have a naturally low nitrogen content are the old two-row barleys that happen to grow particularly well in Britain.

Unfortunately, the best two-row barleys are low in yield and have a low crop density. They require special care during cultivation to keep nitrogen to a minimum: in particular, the use of nitrogen-based fertilisers has to be carefully controlled. In this respect, Britain has a couple of things in its favour: the chalky substrata of the preferred growing region, East Anglia, is low in natural humus and thus nitrogen, simplifying its control. The cool, cloudy, often rainy climate gives the barley a long growing season, which again helps to reduce the nitrogen. During cool, cloudy days when the barley is just ticking over, it is still respiring even though it is not growing particularly rapidly. This helps to use up nitrogen reserves. The high rainfall also helps to leech nitrogen out of the chalky, free-draining soil.

Unfortunately these days, European Union approved crops, farming methods, commercial greed, and many other things are generating a conflict of interests. The requirements for food-grade barley and brewing-grade barley are almost the complete opposite. Barley and malt produced for food purposes or even cattle feed can be high in protein and may even be better off for it. Modern farming methods demand high densities and high yields, and the liberal application of fertilisers is often necessary to achieve this. The traditional low yield, low density, low nitrogen, two-rowed brewing barley is rapidly losing ground to hybrid, high yield, high protein, six-rowed, EU-approved breeds, grown for food or feed use. Many traditional breeds are now "non-approved" under EU rules and "National Lists". It seems that good old-fashioned specialist British brewing barley is rapidly going the same way as the King Edward spud, Cox's apples and bent cucumbers.

Because of this, the traditional British brewing-grade barleys are becoming more expensive and it is becoming increasingly common for British brewers to use malt made from the low-nitrogen fractions of food-grade barley because of its lower price, and it is true that if the maltster selects the barley properly there will not be a problem with protein. Fortunately, some of the traditional breeds, such as Maris Otter, are still being grown.

Many other countries, on the other hand, have (traditionally at least) never had the luxury of indigenous low-nitrogen barley and they have developed special brewing techniques to keep the protein levels in their beer low. The traditional continental methods of brewing lager; under-modifying the malt, the decoction mash, long lagering periods at low temperatures, and post-maturation filtering all have one common aim – to reduce the soluble nitrogen or protein in the beer and maintain clarity. Lager has a special problem because it is usually served highly chilled, is often bottled and thus is expected to have a longer shelf life than draught beers.

Some of the countries that traditionally serve their beers warmer, such as Britain and the Low Countries, still routinely use a number of techniques designed to reduce protein. These include the use of Irish moss, long vigorous boils, the use of low-nitrogen adjuncts (flakes, grits, sugars and syrups), and the use of protein-reducing finings (auxiliary finings, silica hydrogel). Cask-conditioned real ale often has a further advantage in that it is usually consumed before a protein haze has a chance to form.

The reason for this long, if somewhat simplified, discussion on nitrogen and protein is that nitrogen levels feature strongly in the following ingredient descriptions. It is one of the major parameters by which malt is judged, and is more important than many home brewers seem to realise. It determines the appropriate brewing process to be employed, particularly whether or not a simple infusion mash is appropriate.

British-style pale malt is expected to be low nitrogen malt, and, technically at least, is the only type of malt where the traditional, British, single-temperature infusion mash is safe. Continental lager malt is expected to be high nitrogen malt and a protein rest at 50°C (122°F) is considered appropriate during the mashing stage. The protein rest at 50°C breaks down some of the high-order proteins into simpler, less troublesome substances.

Nevertheless, all commercial brewers purchase their malt to a nitrogen specification, irrespective of the actual type of malt being purchased, so there are no hard and fast rules. There are other circumstances that affect things as well, such as whether or not Irish moss is used during the boil, or whether nitrogen diluting adjuncts are used in the grist. The strength of the beer has an effect on the haze potential as well; the amount of protein per pint, so to speak. Obviously a strong beer is more likely to haze than a weak one.

Using nitrogen specifications from a typical maltster, the maximum total nitrogen specifications for his products are as follows: Best Pale Ale Malt = 1.48 per cent; Normal Pale Ale Malt = 1.53 per cent; Best Mild Ale Malt = 1.60 per cent; and Normal Mild Ale Malt = 1.65 per cent. Food-grade malt has a nitrogen content of 1.80 per cent. Of these, the (cheaper) mild ale malts are quite likely to haze with an all-malt beer using an infusion mash, but as mild ales are generally dark in colour, include adjuncts, and are usually fairly weak, the increased nitrogen is not a handicap. The certified analysis of a sample of pale malt (Maris Otter), purchased during the writing of this book, gives an actual, measured nitrogen figure of 1.44 per cent; comfortably within the above specification.

In contrast, the specification for Pilsner and Munich malts (taken from a different maltster's figures) gives the total protein for both as 11 per cent. Using the "6.25" rule gives us a nitrogen content of about 1.75 per cent. An all-malt beer made from malt with 1.75 per cent nitrogen will almost certainly haze if single-temperature infusion mashed, particularly if the beer is to be chilled. However, only about 10 per cent low-nitrogen adjunct (flaked cereals or sugar) would be required in the grist to reduce the total nitrogen to limits capable of being infusion mashed. See the section on mashing for further discussion.

The nitrogen content of coloured, highly roasted, malts; crystal malt, chocolate malt, black malt, etc, is not so important because much of the protein gets destroyed during the cooking process.

USING MALTS

Most malts need to be crushed or cracked before use in the mash tun. Malts can be purchased from home-brew shops either whole or ready crushed. Whole malt is the best bet for those brewers who brew frequently and prefer to buy their malt in bulk, because whole malt keeps better. Adjustable malt mills are available which enable the home brewer to crush his own malt. However, malt mills are expensive, thus for those who purchase their ingredients in smaller quantities it is more convenient and less painful on the wallet to purchase the malt ready crushed.

Your stock of malt should be carefully stored in dry conditions at a fairly stable temperature, particularly crushed malt. Crushed malt absorbs moisture from the air quite readily, becoming what is known as slack. This can cause the malt to lose efficiency and give the danger of throwing a haze.

MALT AND ADJUNCT DESCRIPTIONS

There follows brief descriptions of the ingredients specified in the recipes of this book. All of these, with the exception of peat-smoked whisky malt, are currently available through the British home-brew trade, although there is only one wholesaler that supplies the more specialist, imported continental malts to British shops.

The names applied to malts throughout Europe are often fairly regional. Many countries have different names for virtually identical malts, therefore, to enable people in the greater, wider home-brewing world to choose appropriate malts for any particular recipe, the colour of each ingredient is specified in EBC units; the bigger the number the darker the malt. It is fairly straightforward for those in far-off climes to choose a locally available malt of similar colour rating to achieve a similar beer. Although the colour may be slightly different to that intended, the colour matching of either malt or beer is not a precise science. Indeed, the colour specification of most malts have a very wide tolerance, some of the darker examples have more than a 50 per cent spread (+/−25%), so colour matching is a bit approximate anyway.

American homebrewers, following the methods of the American brewing industry, measure colour in units SRM, whereas the colours of the malts and the resultant beers in this book are in EBC. Generally speaking, it is sufficient to divide the EBC figures by two to arrive at the SRM equivalent. An 30 EBC beer would be about 15 SRM. The two measurement systems are not exactly equivalent, although they use identical (Lovibond) equipment and similar techniques, but to divide by two is as close as we will need.

I have seen published in the American home-brew press a formula designed to convert directly between the two methods, but as much of the stuff written in the home-brew press about beer colour has been technically flawed, I have to treat the formula with suspicion until I have had a chance to check it out for myself. For this reason I have refrained from giving the equivalent SRM colour in the following descriptions or the recipes.

PILSNER MALT
(COLOUR 2.5 EBC)

Usually referred to simply as lager malt in Britain. This is just about the palest malt currently available and, as its name implies, is the stuff used to make pale-coloured Pilsner-style lagers. Pilsner malt is made in just about every European country, but it is named after the town of Pilsen in Czechoslovakia where reputedly, in 1842, the first golden-coloured lager beer was produced.

Pilsner malt is traditionally fairly high in nitrogen cum protein and, technically at least, requires a temperature stepped mash featuring a protein rest period at around 50°C to guarantee a haze free product. Typical specifications for lager malt give a nitrogen content of around 1.75-1.8 per cent. British lager malt from local barley is often lower in nitrogen; 1.6-1.65 per cent.

Some continental lagers exhibit a distinctive sulphury, egg-like flavour and aroma which is produced by chemical known as dimethyl sulphide. The precursors to dimethyl sulphide are contained in the malt, thus it is probably essential to use genuine continental malt and employ a temperature-stepped mash if it is desired to imitate those characteristics.

SCOTCH WHISKY MALT
(COLOUR 2.5 EBC)

This may seem to be a strange thing to include in a book on beer making, but here we have a smoked local malt that has been largely overlooked in home brewing circles. The best quality whisky malts are smoked over peat, providing a rich smoky flavour to the beverage. There is no real reason why the same stuff could not be usefully employed to impart a peaty character to beer. Indeed, the Austrian Eggenberg brewery's flamboyantly named: MacQueens Nessie Whisky-Malt Red Beer, and the French Aldelshoffen brewery's: Adelscott, both use imported Scotch whisky malt to provide a peaty flavour. I have also been reliably informed that some Belgian breweries use the stuff. Why do we let foreigners think of these things first? This is particularly poignant because in the old days, when the majority of malts were smoked as a matter of routine, it is highly likely that the malt used for old-time Scotch ales and Irish ales would have been smoked over plentiful local peat, whereas English malts were smoked over hardwoods, usually hornbeam. The original Guinness malt was certainly smoked over peat.

However, we have to be a little cautious when using whisky malt in brewing because the nitrogen/protein levels are quite high, giving the risk of a haze being thrown. Protein levels are not particularly important to a distillery. However, the specification that I have for whisky malt gives a total nitrogen figure of 1.65 per cent; similar to mild ale malt and a figure we can just about cope with, with careful recipe design. There is unlikely to be any trouble in using whisky malt if a good vigorous 90 minute boil is employed and a generous helping of Irish moss is used during the last fifteen minutes, particularly if the malt is only used as part of the grist or in conjunction with other low protein ingredients; flakes, grits, or sugars. There will not be any problems if a temperature-stepped mash is employed, and, of course, protein levels matter not one iota if a dark beer is being brewed.

PALE MALT

Pale malt is the basis of almost all British beers and many European ones too. This should be high quality, low nitrogen, malted barley, lightly kilned during drying to provide a light colour. British pale malt is made from a number of varieties of barley; Maris Otter, Pipkin, Halcyon, Golden Promise, and others in rough order of preference. Maris Otter is the most highly esteemed of brewing barleys; the most noble and also the most expensive.

Good quality English pale malt, to be used with the traditional single-temperature infusion mash, should be low in nitrogen; having a total nitrogen content of 1.55 per cent or less. Levels much higher than this can give rise to protein hazes developing in the beer or demand the use of a 50°C (122°F) protein rest period during mashing or special fining techniques to maintain clarity, particularly with all-malt beers.

There is an increasing tendency for big British brewers to use cheaper malt containing higher level of nitrogen than formerly and rely on protein-reducing fining aids; Irish moss, auxiliary finings, silica hydrogel, and chill-proofing enzymes; or use nitrogen-diluting adjuncts; flakes, grits, and sugars to maintain the clarity of the finished product.

These days, malt which is good enough for the commercial brewer may no longer be good enough for the home brewer and the poor quality of malt available through the British home-brew trade has been the cause of some concern recently. Home brewers need the very best quality whereas some of the large commercial brewers do not. The trend for some home-brew wholesalers to buy from the cheapest source available has worked to the detriment of the hobby over recent years. The excuse that "it's the same stuff that the mega-brewery down the road uses" is no longer valid; many modern commercial breweries have high-tech brewhouses capable of performing a temperature-stepped mash.

It is important that the home brewer purchases the best quality barley that he can obtain, and from a reputable supplier that can be trusted to give him the quality of malt that his application demands. In fact, good quality malt is no more expensive on the home brewing market than poor quality rubbish, so always insist on the best.

MILD ALE MALT
(COLOUR 7 EBC)

Mild ale malt is a cheaper grade of malt (to commercial brewers) made from barley that has a higher nitrogen content than is usually considered acceptable for ordinary English pale malt. Typical nitrogen levels would be in the 1.6 to 1.65 per cent range. The higher nitrogen content has the benefit of giving mild ale malt a higher diastatic activity than pale malt, but at the expense of extract. The higher diastatic activity assists in the conversion of high levels of adjuncts that are typical of mild ales.

The increased nitrogen content gives the risk of a protein haze being thrown in the finished beer, but as mild ales are usually dark in colour or include other nitrogen-diluting ingredients such as flakes, grits, or sugars, and are usually fairly weak, this is not particularly important.

There is a danger of a haze being thrown if 100 per cent mild ale malt is used to make a strong pale beer. It should be remembered that this malt is intended to be used in conjunction with adjuncts, but only a small quantity of adjunct, ten per cent or less, is necessary to reduce the haze potential of the beer considerably. Higher quantities of adjunct or sugar, or the generous use of protein finings will virtually guarantee a haze free product. The same constraints apply as using whisky malt, see above.

If desired, pale malt can be used as a substitute for mild ale malt in every case, although some references suggest that mild ale malt contributes to the luscious sweetness of milds.

VIENNA MALT
(COLOUR 7 EBC)

This, I suppose, might be regarded as the continental equivalent of British pale malt, although its colour and its nitrogen content are closer to mild ale malt. It is made in the same way as British pale ale and mild ale malts, thus "Vienna malt", as such, is not made by British maltsters although it is available from British home-brew shops via specialist wholesalers. I would suspect that British pale malt or mild ale malt is superior, particularly regarding nitrogen content.

Vienna has a counterclaim to Pilsen in as much as both cities claim to have been the first to make lager. Historically, there has been much bickering between Munich, Vienna, and Pilsen on this point, but all three cities are within a stein's throw of each other, although located in different countries on different sides of the same mountain range. All three share a common brewing heritage and in the 1800s were all working on parallel projects with much collusion between the leading brewers of the three cities. It seems that the first bottom fermented beers were produced in Vienna in 1841, but Pilsen were using bottom working yeasts by 1842 and it seems that Pilsen made the first pale golden-coloured lager in 1842. Anyway, all three cities had the traditional habit of storing their beers in cold mountain caves, which is what lagering is all about.

If old-time Vienna malt was similar to the modern stuff, then early Vienna beers would have been less pale than the British pale ales of the day, which have been around since at least 1710 and were certainly being exported to Europe from the early 1800s onwards. Vienna malt is used by the Germans for making the famous Märzen beers traditionally drunk at the Oktoberfest. If you are unable to obtain Vienna malt, use English mild ale malt, or pale malt failing that.

RAUCHMALZ
(COLOUR 10 EBC)

This is German smoked malt, used to produce the classic Bamberger rauchbiers or smoked beers. This malt is smoked by kilning it over open beechwood fires, giving it a smoky taste and aroma while preserving its diastatic activity. Needless to say, it imparts unique characteristics to a beer; phenols from the wood are absorbed in the malt, giving it its unique flavour.

This malt deserves more attention in Britain as it is an ideal malt for experimentation by those who have an interest in old-style beers. At one time, prior to the early 1800s, just about all British beers were made from smoked malt, smoked over oak, beech, ash, or (usually) hornbeam. Smoked malt gradually lost ground to pale malt during the pale ale revolution of the mid to late 1800s, but many brown ales and porters continued to use smoked malt up until the 1950s. To quote from an old description of brown (smoked) malt being made in Britain in 1870: "The nature of the fuel employed communicates very agreeably the empyreumatic properties that distinguish this class of malt". I couldn't agree more.

MUNICH MALT — LIGHT
(COLOUR 14 EBC)

This is really a darker lager malt, which, as its name suggests, is traditionally used for the sweet beers of Munich. However, like Pilsner malt, it is made in a number of localities, including Britain. Not much else to say about it really, except that it is a darkish flavoursome malt, 14 EBC, and should be multi-temperature or decoction mashed.

MUNICH MALT — DARK
(COLOUR 25 EBC)

A darker version of the above malt, and fairly rare. It is finished at a higher temperature than light Munich malt, and its diastatic power is somewhat lower.

AMBER MALT
(COLOUR 40-60 EBC)

An English malt that is made by kilning mild ale malt at 100-150°C until the desired amber colour is reached. It is then removed from the kiln and allowed to cool. It provides a biscuit flavour and imparts a rich golden colour to beers. Amber malt does have some fermentable sugars but little or no diastatic activity. It must therefore be mashed alongside a diastatic malt, such as pale malt or mild ale malt.

CRYSTAL MALT
(COLOUR 100-300 EBC)

Crystal malt is made in a factory by wetting high-nitrogen malt and holding it at 65°C in an enclosed vessel so that the moisture cannot escape. This mashes the grains and produces a sugary syrup within the husk. Vents are then opened and the temperature is raised to about 250°C which crystallises the sugars and dries and darkens the malt. The grain then consists of a hard sugary mass which readily dissolves in hot water. Crystal malt is high in non-fermentable sugars and therefore provides body and sweetness to a beer, apart from a reddish colour and a pleasant nutty flavour. It does not need to be mashed during use, that has already been done at the manufactory. It is used in the mash tun for convenience, but it can be just as easily be used in the boiler when brewing from malt extract. Crystal malt is available in a whole range of colours, but about 150 EBC is the usual standard.

CARAPILS
(COLOUR 30 EBC)

This is the continental equivalent of crystal malt. Its only major difference is that it is much lighter in colour than British crystal malt. See the above description on crystal malt for further information. It is made in a number of countries, including Britain.

CHOCOLATE MALT
(COLOUR 900-1200 EBC)

Chocolate malt is a malt that has been kilned to a very dark colour. It is used to provide flavour and colour to dark beers: milds, stouts and porters. It imparts a lush sweetish flavour without the intense bitterness or acridity of black malt.

ROASTED BARLEY
(COLOUR 1000-1550 EBC)

Roasted barley is unmalted barley that has been roasted until it is black. It is used to impart a unique dry, burnt flavour to stouts. Being unmalted it is rich in beta-glucans and other head-enhancing components, and its use promotes a thick Guinness-style head. Roasted barley does not need to mashed; it is used in the mash tun for convenience, but it can be used in the boiler when brewing from malt extract.

BLACK MALT
(COLOUR 1250-1500 EBC)

Black malt, as its name implies, is malted barley that has been kilned to a high degree, turning it black. It is used for flavour as well as colour and imparts an astringent sweetness to the beer. If high levels are used it imparts an acrid bitterness. Black malt does not need to be mashed. It is used in the mash tun for convenience, but it can be used in the boiler when brewing from malt extract. It does not really need to be crushed either.

WHEAT MALT
(5 EBC)

Wheat malt is an increasingly popular ingredient in British beers. It supplies a unique flavour and greatly improves head retention. It is used in a number of British beers in small quantities for the reasons mentioned above, and it is a major ingredient in many wheat beers.

CEREAL ADJUNCTS

Cereal adjuncts are used by a number of breweries around the world. Although it is true that adjuncts can be used to produce a marginally cheaper extract than using an all malt grist, their major benefit is as nitrogen diluents. American and Australian brewers, for instance, have to cope with the high nitrogen content of their local six-row barley; 2.2 per cent or even higher. It would be virtually impossible for them to produce a haze free product, capable of being highly chilled, without the use of some additional ingredient to dilute the nitrogen, even though they routinely use a multi-temperature or decoction mash. Fortunately for them, high nitrogen malt is also high in enzymes, the two go together, so their malt can be used to assist in the conversion of very high levels of other low-nitrogen cereals. It is quite usual for American and Australian brewers to use 25-30 per cent rice or maize grits.

Although North European brewers do not have to cope with such high levels of nitrogen, it is quite common, although by no means universal, for them to use smaller quantities of adjuncts as a safeguard against haze. European breweries would typically use only 10 or 15 per cent cereals at most.

GRITS

The basis of a grit is degermed grain. Most of the unwanted nitrogenous matter and oil is contained in the outer layer of the grain; the germ. Grits are made by a two stage milling process which first removes the outer layer of the grain and then mills the remaining endosperm, or kernel, into smaller pieces. Removing the outer layer gives a product that is mostly starch, containing less than 0.1 per cent nitrogen and less than 1.0 per cent oil. Oil, if left in the grain, would interfere with the head formation and retention properties of the beer.

Grits are widely employed by American and Australian breweries, usually rice, maize or sorghum, but are not much used in Europe. The major disadvantage of grits is that they need to be cooked for about 45 minutes before they can be added to the mash tun. This gelatinises the starch, rendering it open to attack by the mash enzymes. Many European breweries, particularly those that infusion mash, prefer to use flaked cereals which do not need the cooking process, but nevertheless have similar properties to the grits. Grits are not generally available on the British home-brew market, but flakes can be directly substituted in any recipe that specifies grits.

FLAKES AND TORREFIED CEREALS

Like grits, flakes and torrefied cereals are made from degermed grain, but they then follow a secondary processing stage which gelatinises the starch. Flakes are made by a wet heat process; by allowing degermed grain to absorb water and swell, either by steaming or soaking, and then passing it through heated rollers. Torrefied grains are made by a dry heat process; by rapidly heating degermed grain, either by microwaves or red hot sand, causing the endosperm to explode, rather like popcorn. In both cases the heat treatment gelatinises the starch, rendering it open to attack by the mash enzymes without further treatment. Both products have low nitrogen and oil content. Flaked cereals and grits are very similar products and interchangeable, except that grits need to be cooked before use, whereas the flakes do not. Torrefied cereals are again very similar products which do not need cooking, but they are said to produce a more nutty flavour, torrefied barley in particular. Flaked rice, flaked barley, flaked maize, flaked wheat, torrefied barley and torrefied wheat are generally available in home-brew shops. Flaked and torrefied cereals can be directly substituted for each other without penalty.

SUGARS

A number of British and European breweries use added copper sugars. Often this is sucrose, cane sugar, usually in the form of invert, although some Belgian brewers use candy sugar, an old form of sucrose crystallised on to string or some other seeding medium. The invert sugar used by British brewers is made from partially refined cane syrup, and therefore does impart some flavour. It is also usually caramelised, which again imparts flavour and also colours the beer.

British brewers have traditionally used invert sugar because they feel that ordinary sugar gives a "sugar tang" to the finished beer and causes disproportionate hangovers. Whether or not this is true is a matter of conjecture, but I can believe it; certainly my own personal experience indicates that it is true. It seems likely that the enzyme invertase, secreted by yeast to invert sucrose, is capable of producing hangovers and can, perhaps, be tasted. Some authorities, however, dispute this.

Although it is true that cane sugar can be beneficial to some recipes, by drying the flavour of a beer, or diluting nitrogen, there is no doubt that a motivation for brewers to use sugar can be to cheapen the extract. Certainly maltose-rich maize syrups that have a similar sugar spectrum to malt, can only be used to cheapen the extract or reduce nitrogen. With British brewers at least, if they used premium quality malt in the first place they would not have a problem with nitrogen – so there is no excuse. Certainly the cheapest form of extract in Britain, and probably Europe as well, is sugar. In some other countries, maize, rice, or sorghum is cheaper.

In general, one of the criteria for selecting beers for inclusion in this book are those that do not use copper sugars, but this has not always been possible to maintain. Some famous names use sugar and it would be churlish to exclude them on idealistic grounds. In some cases the sugar is justified. A strong beer, such as an old ale, may be too sweet and cloying on the palate if it was an all malt recipe, and the use of some sucrose or glucose (being 100% fermentable) would lighten the palate considerably. It also has to be accepted that some breweries may use these additions for technical reasons. Brewers in southern climes would not have access to low nitrogen malt, and may need to dilute the nitrogen of their local malt one way or another; particularly as it seems that the hotter a country's climate, the more the beer is chilled.

Brewers' invert sugar and maize syrups are not generally available through the home-brew trade; although maize-derived crystalline "brewing sugar" is available in some British home-brew shops. Ordinary household sugar can be substituted for invert without penalty. When a particular brewer does use sugar, I have generally specified plain white ordinary household sugar (sucrose). When the brewer appears to use coloured sugar or caramel to darken the beer, I have adjusted for colour using other ingredients, such as dark malts. Caramel has not been specified in any of the recipes, and only neutral-coloured sugar has been specified.

Hops

The varieties and relative quantities of hops employed determine one of the predominant characteristics of any given beer. The hop characteristic of a beer is, perhaps, the most difficult aspect to emulate and provides the most variable aspect of beer production. Hops are the ingredients of the most inconsistent quality in a beer. Not only are different varieties of hop quite different in character, but hop flavour mellows with age and the same variety of hop grown in another region will be subtly different: if it is grown in a different country it can be significantly different. Not only do hops provide bitterness but they also supply aroma and flavour in varying degrees and they can be used at several different stages of the brewing process to impart different characteristics.

BITTERING HOPS

(COPPER HOPS)

Bittering hops are those which are put into the copper at the beginning of the boil to impart the necessary bitterness to the beer. Hops put in at this stage also supply components that act as preservatives and thereby improve the shelf-life. Alpha acid is the primary bittering ingredient of a hop and it follows that hops that are rich in alpha acid are the most economical to use, although any variety of hop can be used for bittering purposes. Indeed, high alpha-acid hops, the most bitter varieties, usually have a harsh flavour and aroma, whereas low-alpha hops, which are less bitter, generally have the best aroma. It is important not to confuse hop flavour with bitterness because they are not quite the same thing.

High-alpha hops are usually hybrids, bred specially for high alpha-acid content and high yields in the hop garden. The high yields make them cheaper to buy and their high alpha-acid make them economical to use as a bittering hop in the copper. The most common bittering hop used in this country is Target, but its flavour and aroma are regarded as unpleasant by many brewers, so it is often used in conjunction with other varieties.

As already mentioned, high-alpha hops usually have a harsh flavour and a poor aroma. In fact, the higher the alpha acid content of the hop, the poorer its flavour and aroma generally becomes. This is not considered to be terribly important by many brewers because much of the flavour and aroma content of the hop is driven off with the steam during the boil, although the bittering and preservative properties remain. It is conventional, for beers that are expected to have a pronounced hop characteristic, to restore the aroma and flavour that is lost by adding a quantity of "aroma hops" to the copper during the last fifteen or twenty minutes of the boil, although not all beers are expected to have a pronounced hop aroma.

AROMA HOPPING

(LATE HOPPING)

It is common practice for both commercial brewers and home brewers to restore lost flavour and aroma by adding a quantity of hops during the last fifteen or twenty minutes of the boil. This is known as late hopping and a quantity of high quality aroma hops, equivalent to about 20-25 per cent of the main batch, is usually employed.

Late hops do not contribute much bitterness to the brew because the short boiling period that they receive does not give enough time for much of the bitterness to be extracted. However, the short boiling period does permit some hop flavour to be extracted (not the same as bitterness), and allows some of the harsher, more objectionable, and fortunately more volatile flavour and aroma components, such as higher hydrocarbons, to be driven off with the steam. Too long a boil, however, and some of the more desirable components may also be driven off.

Only those hops that are considered to have a fine flavour and aroma, usually referred to as aroma hops, should be used at this stage. Traditionally at least, Goldings and Fuggles are considered to be the finest aroma hops for English ales, Hallertau and Saaz varieties for lagers, but because of their relatively high cost (to commercial brewers) many breweries use the new general-purpose hops for all or part of their aroma. Challenger, a Fuggle replacement, is probably the best of the new varieties for this application.

Not all brewers late hop their beers; some of the flavour and aroma from the bittering hops added at the beginning of the boil will be carried across to the final beer and many brewers are content with that. Many beers are expected to have a malty rather than hoppy aroma, thus a second addition of hops for aroma purposes may be contrary to the style. Many people, particularly "learner drinkers", dislike hop bitterness and aroma; it clashes with their youthful sweet tooth. Of course, brewery accountants object to the seemingly wasteful process of chucking in "one for the pot" for no apparent reason (to them).

HOP STEEPING

Another method of imparting additional aroma to a beer is to steep a quantity of hops in the hot wort when the boil is complete and leave it to stand for a period. This is used as an alternative to dry hopping, discussed later. The procedure is similar to late hopping inasmuch as a quantity of the finest aroma hops, equivalent to about 20-25 per cent of the main batch, is added to the boiler either just before or just after the heat is turned off. The infusion is then left to stand for about half-an-hour before the boiler is turned out.

Steeping is said to produce a poorer flavour and aroma than late hopping because some of the more objectionable, harsher components have not had the opportunity to dissipate with the steam, as happens with a short boil. Other critics suggest that some of the more desirable components will not go into solution with a short steep and need a bit of a boil to get them into solution.

Although the characteristics imparted by this method are certainly different to late hopping, probably more aggressive, it is a matter of personal opinion as to whether or not they are "objectionable". It must be said, however, that the technique produces more aroma than flavour, whereas late hopping does introduce some flavour as well. This technique does not add any bitterness to the beer.

At least one old-established British commercial brewer uses a similar method to this, by adding aroma hops to the hop-back before the copper is turned out.

DRY HOPPING

Dry hopping is an old-established method of imparting additional hop aroma to a beer and is the term used to describe the practice of adding a few dry hop cones to the cask during filling; sometimes referred to in commercial brewing as "bung-hole hops". During maturation, essential oils from the hops diffuse into the beer, adding the desired aroma. Again, like the previous methods, dry hopping does not increase the bitterness.

Some objections to dry hopping have been raised: the first is that it takes a few weeks for the full benefit of dry hopping to take effect, and thereafter it can rapidly go past its best, producing a harsh, tannic astringent taste, presumably from the woody parts of the hop. However, this may be more to do with the use of inappropriate hop varieties, or overdoing the application, than any fault of the technique. There is no doubt that only the very best low-alpha aroma hops should be used for dry hopping; any harshness in the hop is bound to reflect in the beer. Unlike late hopping, there is no chance whatsoever of undesirable volatile components escaping to the atmosphere.

Another, perhaps better founded, concern is that adding raw, untreated hops to a cask of beer runs the danger of introducing infection from bacteria living on the hops. With modern low-gravity beers this is indeed a possibility, but I know of nobody who thinks that they have introduced infection in this manner. Nevertheless, home brewers can, if they have concerns about the matter, reduce the likelihood considerably by blanching the hops for a few seconds in a minimal quantity of near-boiling water before adding them to the cask; a stovetop chip-basket and pan is a good gadget for this little job.

Whatever the concerns, the fact remains that commercial brewers were dry hopping before chip-pans were invented, and many of them still do. At least half of Britain's commercial brewers dry hop one or more of their beers by simply shoving raw "bung-hole hops" (or pellets) into their casks. A number of Belgian brewers dry hop, as do one or two German brewers. There is no reason why home brewers should be afraid to do the same.

Quantities employed are a matter of style, but typically range from 8-10 grams per 23 litre batch for weak beers, to as much as 30 grams for strong ales.

INTERMEDIATE HOPPING

This is somewhere in between adding hops at the beginning of the boil and late hopping. As mentioned earlier, the aroma and flavour components of the hop, contributed by hop essential-oils, dissipate with the steam during the boil. However, these flavour compounds are not driven off instantaneously; it takes a good two-hour vigorous boil to drive off most of them. Likewise, the bitterness contributed by alpha acid is not imparted instantaneously. The important reactions take place slowly. It takes time for the alpha acid to be converted into a water-soluble form; the longer the boil the more bitterness is extracted.

Here we have the foundations of a balancing act for certain types of beer: the longer the boil the more bitterness is developed, but more aroma is driven off. There are certain technical benefits to having a long boil, but at the expense of hop aroma. If the hops receive a relatively short boil, however, a proportion of the aroma remains.

About one hundred different constituents have been isolated from hop essential-oils, the stuff responsible for hop flavour and aroma, and many of these get driven off during a long boil. However, not only do they get driven off fairly slowly, but they also seem to get driven off in a particular pecking-order. The most objectionable components get driven off first, or get converted to more pleasing substances during the boil; followed by, mostly, aroma components; and finally what remains of the flavour components. The bitterness remains. This means that as the boil progresses the hop aroma diminishes but, nevertheless, becomes more delicate and pleasing.

This long introduction brings us to another aspect of control, namely the ability to add hops part way into the boil, say half way through, to impart a more delicate and mellow aroma to the beer, perhaps with a less assertive flavour dominating. It also enables less than ideal hops to be used for aroma purposes, with the knowledge that some of the harsher components will be driven off during the short, say 45 minute, boil that they receive.

The technique is not much used by British brewers. In their view, hops at the beginning of the boil for bitterness and top quality aroma hops at the end of the boil is all that should be necessary. However, some continental brewers make a hop addition at the middle of the boil and some make three additions in total; beginning, middle, and end. The intermediate hops generally receive 30-45 minutes of boil time. The quantities employed are generally quite high, usually a similar quantity to the primary bittering hops. They will impart a significant bitterness to the brew, depending upon the length of boil they receive, and this must be accounted for in any bitterness calculations.

There is no point in making more than three additions to the copper, and I know of no commercial brewery that does so, although some American home-brew recipes that I have seen specify half a dozen or so hop additions.

CLASSES OF HOP

As mentioned earlier, high alpha-acid hops are the most bitter, but, generally speaking, their aroma is poor. The aroma of some types of hop is highly prized but with others the aroma is not so good, perhaps even objectionable. This has led to hops being classified, broadly, into three different categories: bittering hops, aroma hops, and general-purpose hops.

Bittering hops are those that are high in alpha acid and are therefore economical to put into the copper at the beginning of the boil to supply the bulk of the bitterness. Any type of hop can, of course, be used for bittering purposes, but a lower quantity of high-alpha hops are needed to achieve the same level of bitterness. For instance, Target, Britain's most widely used bittering hop, contains two-and-a-half times as much alpha acid as Fuggles, therefore two-and-a-half times less Target are required.

Aroma hops are at the other end of the scale. They are those that are generally judged to have the best aroma and flavour, but as a consequence of this, or perhaps coincidentally, they tend also to have a lower alpha acid. Apart from being low in alpha acid, aroma hops are usually charged at a premium price to the commercial brewer. This is because the best aroma hops tend to be the old-fashioned, traditional varieties of hop, such as Goldings and Fuggles, that have low yields, low crop density, and poor disease resistance, making them more difficult to grow. There is no reason why aroma hops should not be used for bittering purposes; indeed, the very best quality beers do. In fact, in the 1950s the Fuggle accounted for more than 80 per cent of Britain's total hop production, indicating that it was the only hop used by the majority of breweries.

General-purpose hops are a stage somewhere between the two. These are modern varieties that are economical to purchase, have a high enough level of alpha acid to provide good bittering properties, but nevertheless have a delicate enough aroma to be useful for aroma hopping. General-purpose hops, such as Challenger and Northdown, are now very widely used; both are grown worldwide. Challenger, in fact, is Britain's second-most widely used hop.

SUBSTITUTING FOR DIFFERENT TYPES OF HOP

The types of hop used in the recipes contained in this book are, where possible, the varieties specified by the breweries concerned, although some substitutions have been made for obscure varieties that are very unlikely to be found in our home-brew shops; "Belgian Star" for example. Almost without exception, the hops actually specified in the recipes are fairly well-known, easily obtainable varieties.

Nevertheless, there is a large number of hop varieties available worldwide and it would be unfair to expect home-brew shops to stock the whole range. There will be times when you will need to substitute one variety of hops for another, either because the specified hops are not in stock, or simply because you wish to experiment or use hops that you already have.

Although much of the character of a beer is dependent upon the hops employed, the substitution of hops is not as serious a departure as it may seem. Few commercial brewers' hop schedules remain static these days. The varieties employed by any particular brewer change almost annually. This is because hops are a very variable commodity, crop characteristics vary considerably from year to year and crop to crop. New varieties are frequently introduced. The very best quality hops require perfect growing conditions and nature does not always oblige. Sometimes yields are low and, from time to time, crops fail completely due to problems with pests.

An international hop market has developed to take advantage of, or perhaps compensate for, regional fluctuations in hop quality, availability and price. Prices fluctuate greatly between the various hop growing regions from year to year. Some varieties of hop can be in short supply and will thus be expensive; whereas there may be a surplus of certain other varieties, perhaps from a different country. Many commercial brewers have the opinion that "alpha is alpha", no matter where it comes from, and they buy their alpha acid from the cheapest source, irrespective of the variety of hop. It is fair to say that this probably makes no difference as far as bittering hops are concerned.

Unfortunately, when substituting different hops, a direct weight-for-weight substitution will not usually provide the same level of bitterness. There is a hop substitution chart given in the appendices to this book, but a simple calculation will also reveal the proper quantity of hops to use. Assuming that you wish to maintain an equivalent level of bitterness, a simple comparison of the alpha acid ratios of the two hop varieties will provide the new quantity of hops. For example; if your recipe calls for 80 grams of Challenger, but you wish to use Goldings instead, the following simple relationship is all that is required.

$$\text{MULTIPLICATION FACTOR} = \frac{\text{Alpha acid of specified hops}}{\text{Alpha acid of substitute hops}}$$

Challenger has an alpha acid of 7.7 per cent and Goldings have an alpha acid of 5.3 per cent. The sum then becomes:

$$= \frac{7.7}{5.3} = 1.45$$

To obtain the new weight of hops simply multiply the quantity of the specified hops by the factor, thus:

NEW WEIGHT OF HOPS   = 80 x 1.45 = 116 grams

Alternatively, using the same figures:

NEW WEIGHT OF HOPS $= \frac{80 \times 7.7}{5.3} = 116$ grams

Many suppliers now print the actual, measured alpha acid of their hops on the packaging, but the typical, average alpha acid content of the most common varieties of hops are listed in table 4.1.

Table 4.1 Average alpha-acids of common hop varieties

Variety %	Alpha Acid	Application
Bramling Cross	6.0	Aroma hop
British Columbian	7.0	General-purpose hop
Bullion	7.9	General-purpose hop
Cascade (USA)	6.0	General-purpose hop
Challenger	7.7	General-Purpose hop
Goldings	5.3	Aroma hop
Fuggles	4.5	Aroma hop
Hallertau*	7.5	Aroma hop
Mount hood (USA)	5.5	Aroma hop
Northdown (seeded)	8.0	General-purpose hop
Northdown (seedless)	10.3	General-purpose hop
Northern Brewer	7.6	General-purpose hop
Omega	9.7	High-bittering copper hop
Progress	6.2	Aroma hop
Saaz (Zatec)*	5.5	Aroma hop
Styrian Goldings*	7.0	Aroma hop (seedless Fuggles)
Target	11.2	High-bittering copper hop
Tettnang	5.0	Aroma hop
Whitbread Golding	6.3	Aroma hop (Fuggles type)
Willamette (USA)	5.5	Aroma hop (seedless Fuggles)
Yeoman	10.6	High-bittering copper hop
Zenith	9.0	High-bittering copper hop

* These are seedless varieties. Because the weight of seeds is not present, seedless varieties have a higher alpha acid than their seeded equivalents (see Northdown). Target is normally grown seeded, but it has a very low seed count.

EUROPEAN BITTERING UNITS
(EBU)

European Bittering Units or, less insularly, International Bittering Units, are a world standard method of assessing the bitterness of beers. Some breweries have provided information on the bitterness of their beers in terms of EBUs and this information has been useful in compiling the recipes. As the rest of the brewing world uses EBUs as an indication of bitterness, it seems appropriate that the home-brew hobby should follow suit.

The bitterness of a beer in EBUs is given by:

$$EBU = \frac{\textbf{weight of hops x alpha acid x utilisation}}{\textbf{volume brewed x 10}}$$

To find the weight of hops required in order to produce a given bitterness in a given volume of beer the formula can be re-written thus:

$$\textbf{WEIGHT OF HOPS} = \frac{\textbf{EBU x 10 x Volume brewed}}{\textbf{alpha acid x utilisation}}$$

Where:

Volume is in litres
Weight of hops is in grams
Alpha acid of hops is in per cent
Hop utilisation is in per cent

HOP UTILISATION

The hop utilisation figure in the equation corresponds to the efficiency of the boil and is dependent upon many things: the vigour of the boil, the length of the boil, the specific gravity of the wort, and the equipment used. In general, the utilisation achieved will be in the range of 20-35 per cent under ideal conditions, with a vigorous one-and-a-half hour boil and the hops boiling freely in the wort.

Because of the variations in methods and technique between home brewers, and the variations in quality of the hops available to us, I have assumed that a typical hop extraction efficiency experienced by home brewers will be at the lower end of this range; namely 20 per cent. All of the recipes in this book are calculated using this figure. This simplifies the equation slightly. Rewriting it to incorporate 20 per cent extraction efficiency:

$$\textbf{WEIGHT OF HOPS} = \frac{\textbf{EBU x volume brewed}}{\textbf{alpha acid x 2}}$$

Therefore to achieve 25 units of bitterness in 27 litres of beer using Golding hops at an alpha acid content of 5.3%:

$$\textbf{WEIGHT OF HOPS} = \frac{25 \times 27}{5.3 \times 2} = 64 \textbf{ grams}$$

This assumes a one-and-a-half hour, good, vigorous boil. EBUs and the American terminology IBUs are exactly the same. They apply only to the bittering hops, i.e., the hops that are put into the copper at the beginning of the boil. Late hops do not contribute much bitterness to the wort due to the shorter dwell time in the copper. They only restore aroma which has been lost during the boil. Late hops are generally 20-25 per cent of the quantity of bittering hops employed, but the exact amount is determined by experience and personal preference.

FORMS OF HOP

Hops are available to home brewers in leaf (whole), plug, and pellet form. Whole hops are the most traditional form and the most appropriate to home brewing. These are the hop cones, or flowers, in their natural state. All the recipes in this book specify whole hops. They can be obtained from home-brew shops loose, but the best samples are available compressed and vacuum-packed in hermetically sealed foil wrappers. This packaging keeps them fresh for much longer periods.

Another stable form of hops, useful to the home brewer, are hop plugs. These are whole hops that have been compressed under high pressure into half-ounce (14 gram) plugs of about one inch (25mm) diameter and then vacuum packed in a foil sachet to preserve them. These expand into whole hops during the boil and behave in exactly the same way. They can be used directly in any recipe in this book. The plugs are a fairly accurate 14 grams, simplifying the weighing of ingredients and the packaging technique seals in freshness.

Pellet hops are hops that have been ground to a powder and then compressed into pellets about 25mm long by about 5mm in diameter. Because pellet hops disintegrate into a powder during the boil they cannot act as a filter bed to filter out the trub after the boil, and are therefore not really applicable to traditional home brewing. It is important not to confuse pellet hops with plug hops, they are not the same thing.

Yeast

INTRODUCTION

Yeast is a difficult subject to treat upon, particularly in a book such as this that draws on beers from all over Europe. Yeast is one of the most important ingredients used in the making of beer; a number of components that go towards the flavour of many beers are supplied by the yeast in the form of fermentation by-products. The quality, flavour, and aroma of a beer are all affected to a certain extent by the type of yeast used.

Yeast is able to convert sugars into alcohol and carbon dioxide. There are various different sugars, or carbohydrates, in our wort. There are simple sugars such as fructose and glucose, and there are more complex sugars such as sucrose and maltose; sucrose being ordinary domestic sugar and maltose being the sugar derived from our malt. Yeast is quite happy to ferment maltose, fructose, glucose and sucrose, and these are fermented into alcohol, disappearing from our wort completely. However, there are also some higher sugars, known as dextrins, that are a group of sugars that brewers' yeast is unable to attack, or is only able to attack very slowly, and thus they remain in our beer and provide body, mouthfeel, maltiness and some residual sweetness.

Brewers' yeasts are fairly specific. They have been trained over a period of several hundred years to enjoy hopped wort and relatively high levels of alcohol; higher levels of alcohol than probably would be found in nature, say by wild yeast fermenting rotting fruit. All brewers' yeasts fall into one of two broad classifications: top working, whereby the yeast rises to the surface of the wort during fermentation; and bottom working, whereby the yeast falls to the bottom of the vat during fermentation.

Top-working yeasts are usually referred to as ale yeasts and are characterised by the forming of a thick fluffy head during fermentation. They work at relatively high temperatures, say 16-20°C (60-68°F), and tend to produce fruity esters and flavour compounds that add to the character of a beer.

Lager yeasts are generally bottom-working yeasts, where most of the yeast settles to the bottom of the vessel during fermentation, although this effect may not be evident in the home-brewing environment. The major characteristic of lager yeast is that it will work at much lower temperatures than its top-working counterpart, say 10-15°C (50-59°F), and produces blander flavours.

The use of the phrases top working and bottom working to denote ale and lager yeasts respectively is rather a gross oversimplification. There are some lager yeasts that produce a fairish head and there are some ale yeasts that produce a poor or no head.

Yeast classification has been in a state of chaos in recent years. At one time ale yeasts were called Saccharomyces cerevisiae and lager yeasts Saccharomyces carlsbergenis. Then, in the 1970s, the microbiologists decided to reclassify lager yeasts as Saccharomyces uvarum; giving the reason that they had decided that S. carlsbergenis did not exist as an independent strain, but instead was a subspecies of S. cerevisiae. But they were still not happy and a few years later they changed their minds again and renamed S. carlsbergenis to Saccharomyces pastorianus and S. uvarum to Saccharomyces bayanus.

Now, to cap it all, they have changed their mind yet again. Genetic fingerprinting or DNA mapping has shown that things are not quite as they thought. Strains that have hitherto been regarded as separate have turned out to be identical and the distinction between top-working and bottom-working yeast is not as clear-cut as was once imagined. Currently all brewing yeasts are lumped under the Saccharomyces cerevisiae label, with the subdivisions "ale" or "lager" based on typical application rather than on any morphological differences; at least until the DNA mapping exercise is complete. They didn't have me fooled for one moment!

The reclassification of brewers' yeasts by DNA mapping does have some interesting implications. It seems likely that the 3000 or so yeast strains currently held in various national yeast collections may be reduced to a few hundred that are proven, genetically, to be independent strains.

SOURCES OF YEAST

It is probably true to say that to emulate fully any particular beer it would be necessary to use the same yeast that the brewery concerned uses, but having said that, perfectly acceptable results will be obtained in most cases by using yeasts commonly available on the amateur market. The only difficulty may arise if a particular yeast imparts an unusual, distinguishing characteristic, such as sourness. The Rodenbach yeast is a particular example; it consists of a mix of about twenty strains, some of which are souring. Some of the German wheat beer yeasts seem to produce a slight sourness, as does, in my view, Wadworth yeast. Some German wheat beers are deliberately inoculated with a lactobacillus strain. Lambic, of course, is a classic example of a soured beer, the sourness being imparted by secondary, wild(?) yeasts, although I cannot see that they should be considered as wild if one is actually encouraging them to grow.

With most of the heavily soured beers, such as Lambic or Rodenbach, the sourness is imparted by secondary yeasts which become active during lengthy maturation. With these beers it is perfectly acceptable for primary fermentation to be conducted using a standard ale yeast. Most Lambic brewers give their beers a helping hand by starting their beers with a top-working ale yeast, despite their insistence on "spontaneous fermentation". It is, in fact, only the secondary fermentation, that is, or indeed needs to be, "spontaneous", caused by "wild" yeasts. Most of the soured beers originated way back in history, and old-time brewers did not use the term "secondary fermentation" in the same way that we do today. In the old days it literally meant a vigorous secondary fermentation in cask, caused by secondary yeasts – different strains to the primary yeast. It did not mean mere "conditioning" as is the usual understanding today.

After an intentionally sour beer has been started using a standard ale yeast, it is then possible to encourage the appropriate secondary yeasts to set up residence, either gathering them from the atmosphere or from raw grain. Many of these yeasts, and other micro-organisms, are naturally present on barley and wheat and they can be cultured from this. Despite the rich cocktail of micro-organisms present, only the appropriate ones will survive in the beer because the conditions imposed by any given beer style; hop rate and alcohol levels in particular, will be selective towards the important micro-organisms; the others will die or be inhibited. In olden times, when most of these beer styles originated (1500s in some cases), brewers did not have much in the way of microbiological methodology available to them. It was the conditions set up in the beer that determined which micro-organisms were going to be active, and thus the beer style. More information on soured beers will be found in one of the appendices.

As regards ale yeasts, some types produce fruity esters that give the beer a fruity aroma and aftertaste, and some types are said to produce more esters than others. However, the conditions prevalent in the wort, pH, temperature, and oxygen levels probably have more effect on ester formation than the yeast strain itself. Most yeasts produce fruity esters given the right conditions.

Lager yeasts are much more straightforward. The majority of lagers have little, if anything, in the way of distinguishing flavours supplied by the yeast. The colder temperatures at which lager is usually fermented inhibit the production of esters and other flavour by-products of fermentation. However, not all lagers are fermented at cold temperatures. With some of the traditional lagers produced in old Czechoslovakia and Bavaria, the primary fermentation is conducted at relatively high, ale-like temperatures in open fermenters; it is only the lagering period itself that takes place in the cold.

DRIED YEAST

Although the type of yeast employed can have a great influence on the character of the beer, good quality dried yeast is adequate for many of the beers in this book. The major problem with dried yeast is that not very many different types are available and often the packagers are reluctant to state what strain of yeast is actually contained in the packet. The economics of growing and drying large enough quantities of yeast to justify running an automatic packaging machine do not allow for many different varieties to be produced for what is, after all, a fairly small market in national terms.

Paradoxically, lager brewers seem to be better catered for than ale brewers in Britain. A fairly good range of dried lager yeasts are available and some packagers give the type or source of the yeast. However, the authenticity of some of the ale yeasts is questionable, to the extent that there are only two or three brands that I would trust to be true top-working ale yeasts. This mistrust is supported by the packagers' reluctance to disclose what is actually in the packets. Nevertheless, some brands are reliable; I have tested both SB12 and Gervin ale yeasts and have found them to perform true to type; with SB12 probably being the most vigorous of the two.

However, do not trust a packaged yeast that is merely labelled as "Beer Yeast" or "Brewer's Yeast". This can mean anything, and with something labelled so non-committally it probably will be. Ensure that the package states clearly that it is a lager yeast if you intend to brew a lager, or an ale yeast or "real ale" yeast for good quality English ales.

Most packets contain only five grams of yeast and the viability of dried yeasts is such that a large proportion of this will be dead cells. Many strains of yeast do not survive the drying process too well, although some strains are more robust than others. However good the viability of the yeast may be, five grams, in my opinion, is nowhere near enough to ensure a reliable start to a five gallon brew. It is almost essential to make up a yeast starter culture if good results are to be achieved. Another benefit, according to American home brewing experience, is that beer flavour is much improved by pitching with an adequate quantity of active yeast. Using too small a quantity can, apparently, produce undesirable off-flavours in a beer.

For those who do not want to make a starter culture, or for some reason are unable to make one up, best results will be achieved if the dried yeast is rehydrated before use and if two or three packets are used rather than one. To rehydrate the yeast, sterilise a cup and saucer and then dissolve the yeast in about half a cupful of lukewarm water at a temperature of about 35°C (95°F) and leave to stand for about fifteen minutes, covered with the saucer. After the standing period the yeast can be added to the wort.

LIQUID YEASTS

The ability to select an appropriate yeast for the type of beer being brewed can have an influence on authenticity when trying to emulate a commercial beer. Liquid yeast goes some way to providing that ability, for the simple reason that liquid yeasts can be made available in a far wider range of types and strains than is possible with the more conventional dried yeast.

Various liquid yeasts appear on the British home-brew scene from time to time, but they tend to come and go with surprising rapidity. British home brewers do not seem to have readily accepted liquid yeasts, which is a pity, because they enable pure yeast of laboratory quality to be made available to amateur brewers. Apart from the fact that liquid yeast from a reputable supplier will perform true-to-type and be virtually bacteria free (a quality that is not usually the case with dried yeasts), another great advantage of liquid yeasts is that they enable specialist strains, and strains specific to certain styles of beer, to be supplied fairly readily; strains that would be uneconomic, due to the small volumes involved, to propagate dry and package in the conventional sense.

The term, liquid yeast, is a bit of a misnomer inasmuch as it is really a small quantity of bacteriologically pure, active yeast in a liquid medium. They are usually supplied in screw-capped sterile plastic tubes containing 20-30 millilitres of liquid medium. The quantity of yeast actually contained in them is quite small, only milligrams, so a yeast starter culture certainly is essential, but the viability and vigour of the yeast is such that it usually takes no longer for the starter to become active than when using standard dried yeast. As any serious home brewer always makes a yeast starter prior to brewing anyway, there is no real handicap or difficulty in using liquid yeasts.

Although liquid yeasts have not been a great success in Britain, in America it is a different story; American home brewers have taken to them quite enthusiastically and they have three or four manufacturers supplying them with a very wide range of different strains and varieties.

Some suppliers have attempted to import the American liquid yeasts into Britain, but several of the imported examples tended to be of extremely poor viability and took ages to get started in a culture medium; several days with some examples I experimented with. This, I suspect, probably had more to do with their journey across the Atlantic than any fault with the yeast itself. If the yeast is allowed to freeze, say in an unheated cargo-hold of an aircraft, or conversely allowed to get too hot, its viability will be severely impaired. Anyway, certain brands of liquid yeast of American origin disappeared as suddenly as they arrived.

WYEAST
LIQUID YEASTS

One home-brew wholesaler is currently importing the Wyeast range of liquid yeasts from America. Wyeast is quite unique inasmuch as it comes complete with its own in-built starter system. It is ingeniously packaged in a two-part foil sachet, one part contains about 50 ml of culture medium and the other part contains the yeast; the two are kept separate by an inner membrane. To use the yeast the inner membrane is broken by kneading the sachet and it is left for a day or two for the yeast to multiply. As the yeast grows the sachet swells and at this point the yeast is ready to use.

Wyeast suggest that sufficient yeast is produced to enable it to be pitched directly into the wort, but the in-built 50 ml starter is not really enough; a good 250-300 ml is required for predictable results with a 25 litre batch of beer. This means that even this clever system requires a yeast starter culture to be made up before brewing. It would probably be quicker in the long run to use a conventional phial of pure liquid yeast in conjunction with a starter culture. Some American home brewers performed tests using Wyeast with and without a starter and published their results on the Internet. The conclusion was that using it in conjunction with a yeast starter gave by far the best results.

A great advantage of Wyeast is the extremely wide range of different yeasts available; the British importer is currently stocking about sixteen of them. Wyeast are as reluctant as their British counterparts to disclose the exact source of their yeast, but they give a sufficient number of clues to enable an appropriate selection to be made; descriptions such as English ale, Irish ale, Bavarian weizen, Munich lager, etc. According to the importer's literature, it seems that these too can sometimes be a bit sluggish to start; samples close to the best before date can take four days or longer to reach pitching condition.

ALEMASTER ZYMOPURE
LIQUID YEASTS

These seem to be Britain's countermeasure to the invasion of American liquid yeasts, and I must say that importing English ale yeast from America does seem to be like selling sand to the Arabs. The Alemaster Zymopure range are conventional liquid yeasts, produced in Britain, and supplied in screw-capped sterile tubes containing about 25 millilitres of active medium. A useful feature of Alemaster yeasts is that the sources are specified. The yeasts are sourced from named breweries or their products, by fair means or foul, and they are then isolated, purified, and grown up in a commercial propagator under sterile conditions before packaging.

Due to the small size of the UK market for this type of product, Alemaster yeasts are not available in the wide variety of strains that some American manufacturers, such as Wyeast, supply. Alemaster overcomes this problem by supplying a standard range of about a dozen yeasts covering most generic beer styles, English ale, Bavarian wheat beer, Belgian ale, Pilsner lager, etc, with some of the donor breweries changing occasionally. This is supplemented with a series of "guest" yeasts that change from time to time. This means that the range of yeasts available will change regularly, but it seems to be a sensible method of supplying the widest possible range. Yeasts from popular breweries, Fullers, Brakspears etc, are available on a virtually permanent basis.

These yeasts show signs of activity in a matter of hours after adding to a starter solution and their long-term viability is excellent when stored under proper conditions. Alemaster yeasts have a six months "best before" date, but seem to maintain excellent viability well beyond that. In recent tests some phials of their Fullers-type yeast were deliberately allowed to go past their best-before date and were also roughly treated during this period. The rough treatment consisted of taking them out of the refrigerator and leaving them out for days on end before putting them back, shaking them up and all sorts of mischievous tricks of that nature. Eventually these yeasts were cultured up in 250 ml starter solutions at nine p.m. one night, and by eight o'clock the following morning they had acquired a fair sized yeast head and the airlocks were "blooping" well. Later analysis proved them to be bacteriologically sound too. This is an impressive performance, although it may be that some strains of yeast are more resilient than others when subjected to this sort of treatment.

CARE AND STORAGE OF LIQUID YEAST

Liquid yeasts require careful storage conditions if they are to remain sound. They must be kept refrigerated, at a temperature above 4°C; they should not be frozen. The maximum density of water occurs at about 4°C, and the expansion if taken below this will rupture the cells. The salad drawer in most refrigerators is usually the best place to keep them, this will usually be maintained at the right sort of temperature because lettuces and other vegetables go "squidgy" if the temperature falls below 4°C. Some liquid yeasts are designed to be kept in the freezer, but these will contain an antifreeze of some sort; glycerin, glycerol, glycol, or alcohol. Yeast spores will survive freezing, but the main vegetative cells will not.

Ensure that the shop proprietor stores the yeast properly too. I have seen them displayed on open shelves at ambient temperatures in some homebrew shops, and this won't do them much good at all. The yeasts can stand a few days at ambient temperatures without coming to much harm, when purchasing them mail order for example, but they should be popped into the fridge on arrival. Liquid yeasts are produced under sterile conditions; the bacteria count is very low, close to zero, so they are unlikely to "go off" readily. However, the viability of the yeast falls with time as the yeast cells gradually die off, the higher the temperature, the faster this happens.

Liquid yeasts generally have a best before date of six months from manufacture. This is perfectly adequate as long as they have been stored properly by the wholesaler, retailer, and home brewer alike. Generally, the closer the age of the yeast is to its best before date, the longer it takes for the yeast to become active in the starter medium, but nevertheless, activity is usually apparent within hours, even with time-expired yeasts. Normally it should be sufficient to make a yeast starter 24-48 hours before you intend to brew. If a yeast takes longer than three or four days to show activity, this indicates that the vegetative yeast cells have been killed somehow or have died of old age, and only the spores have survived. The spores will survive almost indefinitely and can be cultured up, but, nevertheless, something is wrong with the quality if this happens.

Do not be tempted to open the phial until you are ready to use the yeast. The manufacturer goes to a lot of trouble to keep bacteria out and his effort will have been wasted if you let it back in again. It will keep nowhere near as well once you have opened the phial. Remove the sample from the fridge and allow it to warm to room temperature before you use it. It is usually sufficient to do this at the same time you begin to make up the yeast starter. Shake the phial to get the yeast into suspension, remove the cap and tip into your starter solution.

I have seen instructions given for re-using yeast reclaimed from primary fermentation as a method of reducing the cost of the relatively expensive liquid yeast cultures. The technique advocated involves separating the yeast from the sludge after fermentation by floating it on water and then keeping the yeast in a jar in the fridge. They claim that the yeast will last for up to a month. Although this technique is rumoured to have originated from an American yeast supplier, I feel that the risk of ending up with contaminated yeast is too great for the method to be practical. At best, I would expect the beers produced from this yeast to have a drastically reduced shelf-life if the yeast is kept for more than about a week.

A safer method would be to make up a yeast starter prior to making a brew and inoculate the starter with a new pure liquid yeast. When the starter is ready, and before adding it to the main brew, tip 20-30 millilitres of it into a small sterile bottle or the tube the yeast was originally supplied in and pop this into the fridge. This secondary sample can then be used in the same way as your original phial of liquid yeast when you next brew. Take extra care over cleanliness and sterilisation when preparing for this operation and be sure to use an airlock on the starter. The best thing to fill the airlock with, in my view, is hydrogen peroxide, the stuff sold in chemist shops for bleaching hair. Use it neat from the bottle (it comes as a 3-5% solution) and be careful not to overfill the airlock.

No matter how careful you are, you will always get some bacteria into your secondary yeast sample. The stuff is all around us in the air, it's on our hands, in our hair, and we breathe the stuff out. The secondary sample will not keep anywhere near as well as the commercially made, pure sample that you purchased. However, it should keep okay for a month, and it should be safe to use up to then. Never make a third generation from your secondary yeast sample; the risk of making a bacteria starter instead of a yeast starter increases exponentially each time you do this. You can, of course, make more than one secondary sample from your original pure yeast, but you must use it within a month.

STEALING YEAST FROM A BOTTLED BEER

It is quite possible to culture yeast from the dregs of certain types of bottled beer and this is a useful method of obtaining some of the yeasts used by the breweries mentioned in this book. Only beers that have not been pasteurised or sterile-filtered are useful in this way. Pasteurisation is a heat-treatment that kills the yeast and sterile-filtration is a micro-pore filtering process that removes the yeast; either way no viable yeast is present. Only what I call, live bottled beers are suitable for yeast culturing.

A number of European breweries export live bottle-conditioned beers to various countries, but the problem is knowing which they are. Unfortunately, the breweries are not consistent in the matter. In some of my previous writings I provided a small list of live beers available in England from which yeast could be recovered, but I then received several letters from correspondents in foreign parts, describing tales of woe and of failure to culture yeast from some of the beers mentioned. On further investigation I discovered that whether any particular beer is available in any particular country in a live or sterile form is rather arbitrary, based on marketing policy and sometimes local legislation. A beer that may be available live in one country is sterile in another. There are even differences between Scotland and England. Determined not to fall into the same trap again, this time I will not make any suggestions other than you suck it and see. It does not cost a fortune to buy a couple of bottles of beer for experimental purposes, and you get to drink the beer anyway.

A few hints and tips, however, may help you to choose likely candidates: Unlike cask ales, few British bottled beers are available in live form, most are pasteurised, but those that are live will make a big thing about it on the packaging as a consequence of Britain's "real ale" culture. However, the fact that a beer is claimed to be bottle-conditioned and contains a yeast sediment does not mean that it is live. Some breweries bottle-condition the beer, but when conditioning is optimum they run the bottles through a tunnel pasteuriser (hot water pasteuriser) to stabilise the beer.

Pilsner-style beers are almost universally sterile-filtered; it is considered an essential part of the Pilsner process by many breweries. Some are pasteurised too to make doubly sure. However, getting hold of good Pilsner yeast from commercial sources is fairly easy these days. Almost all well-known German beers are filtered too. Sterile filtration of beer was invented in Munich, and they have been doing it for, perhaps, a century or more. For a German brewer to filter his beer is as natural to him as putting hot water in his mash tun. The traditional Diatomatious Earth (Diatomite) filter medium is referred to in the brewing industry by the German term "kieselguhr" (the "guhr" suffix, strangely enough, means fermentation). Another well-known German brewing term "Krausen" only came about because, before counter-pressure bottling machines were invented, the Germans needed to put some yeast back into the beer after the filtering stage for conditioning purposes. It was a necessary step for technical reasons; it had nothing whatsoever to do with the Reinheitsgebot, as I have often seen expounded by homebrew writers. A large number of German beers contain no viable yeast, and with some of those that do, the beer is usually filtered and re-yeasted, sometimes with a different strain to that used for primary fermentation. Successfully culturing yeast from German beers could be very much a lottery without an intimate knowledge of German brewing. Nevertheless, Germany has hundreds of breweries and it is possible to culture the yeast from many of the specialist beers.

In contrast, anyone trying to culture yeast from the beers of Belgium, or the Low Countries in general, would have a very high success rate. The majority of Belgian beers are available live, and the Belgian breweries are more consistent regarding their foreign policy. I have successfully cultured yeast from Chimay, Orval, and one or two others, and I know that American and Australian home brewers have achieved similar successes with the same products available in their countries.

A CAUTIONARY NOTE

It would be wrong to suggest that the yeast used by the respective commercial brewery is always the appropriate choice for a home brewer. Some commercial brewery yeasts are quite badly behaved in the home-brew environment. Some of those used by large commercial brewers are selected to perform well in tall conical fermenters under high concentrations and high hydrostatic pressure; they would not work particularly well in shallow home-brew vessels. The yeasts used by brewers who filter or centrifuge their beers may not clear down readily. Some yeasts require rousing every few hours to maintain sufficient yeast in suspension, some require regular aeration too. Busy working people do not normally have the opportunity to do this, although a small circulation pump will usually overcome this problem. Other yeasts are fairly unstable, and mutate easily, requiring frequent reculturing to maintain viability.

Another potential problem is related to the small depth of the fermentation vessels used in home brewing. During fermentation yeast usually moves up and down through the beer, being carried up when it produces a bubble of carbon dioxide, and sinking back through the beer after releasing its bubble, picking up more nutrients on the way down. The fermentation vessels of most old traditional breweries are about six feet deep, this being the depth that Victorian brewing scientists thought was optimum. The small depth of home brewing vessels means that the yeast does not have very far to travel, and as a consequence it spends most of its time sitting in a heap on the bottom of the vessel. Some yeasts stop working when they sediment, whereas others maintain activity. Nevertheless, the efficiency of any yeast is probably impaired when he has several million of his colleagues sitting on top of him.

MAKING A YEAST STARTER CULTURE

It is almost essential to make up a yeast starter culture prior to any brewing session. The small quantities supplied in commercial yeast packages are not sufficient to ensure a healthy start to the fermentation of a twenty-five litre or five gallon brew. The average package of dried yeast contains only about five grams, which is nowhere near enough; liquid yeasts contain even less. It is essential that our beer is supplied with a adequate quantity of active yeast to ensure that it is able rapidly to establish itself and form a protective head before bacteria have a chance to gain a foothold.

Brewers' wort is a perfect culture medium, rich in all sorts of nutrients, vitamins and minerals. All manner of little "nasties" are quite happy to breed in it and will do so if they are given the opportunity. Once the yeast is established, however, its in-built defence mechanism keeps most forms of bacteria at bay. It is in your interest to get the yeast established at the earliest possible point.

A yeast starter culture takes only a few minutes to make up. It is made a couple days before you plan to brew and ensures that you have an adequate quantity of active yeast grown under relatively sterile conditions before you begin. This minimises the risk of problems with yeast performance or infection. The lag phase, i.e., the time between pitching the yeast and something starting to happen, is reduced considerably because the yeast has converted to aerobic respiration and is actively multiplying before it is pitched.

It is important to ensure that a yeast starter does not inadvertently become a bacteria starter as well. Therefore it is essential that a starter is prepared under conditions of the greatest sterility that we are able to achieve. This is not going to be particularly great in a domestic environment, but a combination of chemical sterilisation and heat will provide an adequate level of sterility.

I often use a standard, "dumpy" style, one-pint milk bottle as a culturing flask because it is designed to withstand boiling water and it will accept a wine-maker's airlock and rubber bung, although some styles only accept a half-gallon bung. Ordinary returnable beer bottles (meaning not disposables) are also designed for hot water sterilisation and I have also used these successfully. They will not take an airlock easily, but a wad of cotton-wool pushed into the neck will act as a bacteria trap.

So far I have had no accidents caused by transferring boiling fluids to these bottles, but the possibility exists that the bottle may shatter. Please exercise the utmost caution when messing around with boiling fluids and glass – a nasty combination.

Making a yeast starter is straightforward enough:

1. Sterilise a one-pint bottle, an air lock, a rubber bung, and a small funnel using Alemaster Knackerbug, Chempro SDP or similar. After sterilisation rinse the items very thoroughly. Preheat the bottle with hottish water and then fill it with boiling water from the kettle and leave it to stand.

2. Bring approximately half a pint (250 ml) of water to the boil in a saucepan and then add four generous tablespoons of malt extract (50-60 grams). Simmer for a couple of minutes or so, stirring continuously to avoid burning, and then turn off the heat.

3. Carefully empty the hot water from the bottle and then pour in the hot malt-extract solution via the funnel. The bottle should be about half full. Cover the mouth of the bottle with a piece of aluminium kitchen foil and stand it in a bowl of cold water until it has cooled to room temperature. The solution will cool faster if the bottle is given a shake from time to time in order to redistribute the contents.

4. When the solution has cooled, and with the foil still covering the mouth of the bottle, give it a vigorous shake to admit oxygen into the solution.

5. When you are sure that the solution has cooled to room temperature, add your yeast, give the bottle a final vigorous shake, fit the sterilised bung and air lock, and stand the starter in a warmish place of about 20-25°C. Ensure that the outside of the bottle is clean and free from malt extract solution as this will be a potential bug trap.

Do not brew your main batch of beer until you are sure that the yeast is actively fermenting. This will be indicated by the typical frothy head developing and carbon dioxide bubbles propagating through the airlock. The time taken for the starter to become sufficiently active for pitching is dependent upon yeast viability, initial quantity of yeast, and temperature. Normally activity occurs within a few hours and the yeast will have grown to a suitable volume in 24-48 hours. When culturing yeast from a commercial bottled beer it can take several days for activity to show. Normally, if you intend to brew on a Sunday morning you would probably make your yeast starter on a Friday night; it can be kept under airlock for a few days until you are ready to brew.

If you are fortunate enough to have access to a Pyrex laboratory flask, a more professional method of producing a yeast starter medium is to add the water and malt extract to the flask and heat the flask directly, simmering the contents for about a minute. Cover the mouth of the flask as above, and cool the flask with cold water. When the flask has cooled to room temperature, add the yeast, shake, fit airlock etc. You may be tempted to put the malt extract and cold water into a bottle or flask and boil it in one hit in the microwave oven. At first thought this seems an ideal way of achieving ultimate sterility, but apparently it is a very dangerous practise. Boiling in the microwave generates super-heated zones in the liquid which can cause the contents of the bottle to erupt like a volcano as soon as it is disturbed, with disastrous consequences. Sticky super-heated fluids sprayed over one's person cannot be much fun, so if you must do it – please be careful. Certainly leave a considerable period of time between switching off the microwave and removing the solution from the oven.

Dried malt extract is available from your home-brew shop and is more convenient than malt extract syrup when used for this application. Dried malt extract should be stored very carefully and in a dry place because it will absorb moisture from the atmosphere and set in a hard lump, like toffee. I store mine in air-tight Kilner jars (yes they are still available), Americans call them canning jars I think. An air-tight sandwich box would do just as well. If your dried malt extract does happen to set hard, simply break it up with a suitably sized whacking implement. It will still be perfectly suitable for yeast propagation purposes.

RECOVERING YEAST FROM A BOTTLED BEER

As mentioned earlier, lifting yeast from a bottle of commercial beer is one way of obtaining specialist yeasts. The procedure is quite simple.

1. Stand the donor bottle in a cool place and leave it undisturbed for a day or two to allow the yeast to settle to the bottom.

2. Make up a yeast starter using stages 1 to 4 of the procedure described above.

3. When the starter has cooled to room temperature, carefully uncap the donor bottle and decant all but the last half-inch of the contents into a glass, taking care to ensure that any yeast sediment is left behind in the bottle.

4. Give the remaining contents of the donor bottle a good shake in order to dislodge any yeast clinging to the bottom of the bottle. Tip the entire contents, dregs and all, into the yeast starter solution. Shake, fit a sterilised airlock, stand in a warm place etc, as above.

5. Drink contents of glass.

Some commercial beers have a very low residual yeast count and it may take several days for signs of activity to show in the starter medium. Some types of yeast pack firmly down on to the bottom of the bottle. With these types it may be necessary to pour the solution from the starter into the donor bottle, shake and pour back into the starter repeatedly until the yeast has been dislodged.

WORT AERATION REQUIREMENTS OF YEAST

There is insufficient space in a book such as this to address many of the technical aspects of yeast, but a brief mention of the aeration requirements of yeast is justified because many home brewers seem to be afraid to aerate their wort, probably because many early home brewing books advocated keeping air away from beer, almost to the point of paranoia.

Brewers' yeast has two methods of respiration, aerobic (with oxygen), and anaerobic (without oxygen). Not all yeasts have the ability to respire by these two different methods, but all brewers' yeasts must have this ability. Yeasts that are able to change from one form of respiration to another are known as facultative anaerobes. A brewers' yeast prefers to respire aerobically if given the opportunity, and will do so if the medium in which it is working has a plentiful supply of dissolved oxygen. However, when the supply of dissolved oxygen is used up the yeast will revert to anaerobic respiration, whereby it synthesises its oxygen from the medium in which it is working.

When the yeast is first pitched it respires aerobically utilising the dissolved oxygen in the wort. During this aerobic phase the yeast multiplies at an exponential rate and very quickly establishes itself. To ensure that this preliminary rapid growth phase takes place the brewer must ensure that the wort is well aerated before, or at about the same time as, the yeast is pitched, because the yeast will only multiply significantly if it is permitted to respire aerobically. When the dissolved oxygen in the wort has been used up, the yeast is then forced to revert to anaerobic respiration. Reproduction noticeably slows down as the yeast adapts itself to anaerobic respiration. The yeast always finds it a bit of a struggle to respire anaerobically, but it is only under anaerobic conditions that alcohol is produced. This brings us to an important point that is not often made clear in many home-brewing books:

At the time that the yeast is added (pitched) it is important that the wort is well aerated, has a plentiful supply of dissolved oxygen, but once the yeast has established itself it is just as important that care is taken to ensure that a minimum of air gets into solution from that point on, except, perhaps, for certain corrective measures such as yeast rousing.

The boiling phase of beer-making drives off any dissolved air that may be present. It is therefore necessary to aerate the wort after it has cooled. This can be done either by sloshing the cooled wort from one brewing bin to another, creating plenty of mechanical action; or, my preferred method, simply running the wort from one bin to another using the fitted tap, via a fairly lengthy airborne drop. If you only have one brewing bin, vigorously stirring the wort; or using a small saucepan as a baler, and sloshing the wort around with that, will help to aerate. If the wort foams you are getting air in.

Mashing methods

INTRODUCTION

Mashing is the process whereby the fermentable sugars are extracted from our malt grain and adjuncts. A wide variety of mashing methods are used throughout Europe. It is assumed that the reader has some mashing experience. The following description can only outline techniques and propose certain suitable home brew methods, the reader is directed to one of the many books on home brewing to obtain more complete information; preferably one with Wheeler printed somewhere on the cover.

INFUSION MASH

The simple, single-temperature infusion-mash is the system used by the majority of British, Belgian and some German brewers. It is the easiest and probably the best of the various mashing methods. Basically, it consists of steeping the grain in hot water at a temperature of about 65°C and allowing it to stand for up to ninety minutes. During this standing period, the enzymes in the malt convert the starch contained in the pale malt and in the other ingredients into various types of sugar.

Commercial breweries that infusion mash usually use an unheated, well-insulated mash tun that has a perforated false bottom to retain the grain so that the wort can easily be drained from the mash. The vessel relies on good heat insulation to maintain the temperature so a heater is not required. The overriding requirement is that the tun is capable of holding the temperature of the mash reasonably constant over the ninety minute typical mashing period.

The mash is performed by charging the mash tun with hot water at strike heat, about 75°C (167°F), at the rate of about two litres of water per kilogram of grain. Once the temperature of the tun has stabilised, and the water readjusted to strike heat, the grain is stirred in. This will cause the temperature of the mash to drop close to initial heat.

When all of the grist has been introduced to the tun it should be very thoroughly stirred to ensure that there are no dry pockets, which would cause inefficiency, and a check on temperature should be made to ensure that it is at the desired initial heat. If it is not, it should be adjusted as quickly as possible by adding boiling or cold water, while stirring, until the temperature is correct. Initial heat can be anywhere between 61°C and 68°C (142-155°F) and give good results, but for most beers it is probably best to aim for 65-67°C (149-153°F). High temperatures produce a dextrinous wort which will produce a beer rich in body but slightly lower in alcohol, whereas lower temperatures produce a drier, but more alcoholic beer.

Once correct conditions have been ascertained, the lid should be fitted to the mash tun and thermal insulation placed over the lid. It should then be left to stand for the appropriate mashing period, usually one to one-and-a-half hours. After the standing period the mash is run off and sparged in the normal manner.

THE DECOCTION MASH

The decoction mash is a mashing technique, traditionally used for the production of lager, which was developed by the Germans in the mid-nineteenth century in order to cope with undermodified, high nitrogen malt at a time when clear, pale beers were becoming fashionable; probably as a result of the export success of British pale ales.

The local malt available to German brewers was less than suitable for producing pale, clear beers. Unlike British two-rowed pale malt, the malt of mainland Europe was excessively high in nitrogen and therefore prone to throwing a protein haze in the beer, although I doubt if either British or German brewers realised that nitrogen levels were the secret.

The Germans developed a number of techniques to overcome this haze problem. In fact, all the techniques that are applied to the production of lagers; undermodified malt, decoction mash, long lagering periods at low temperatures, and keisleguhr filtering, all have one simple goal – to reduce the nitrogen cum protein levels in the finished beer and thereby produce a beverage that is clear and remains clear when chilled.

The term "decoct" means to prepare by boiling. A decoction mash is started at low temperature, 40 or 50 degrees C, and the temperature is gradually raised in a step-wise fashion by frequently removing a proportion of the mash, say a third, boiling it, and then returning it to the main mash. The main features of a decoction mash are a low-temperature protein rest period at 45°C to 55°C, and the regular boiling of a fraction of the mash.

The protein rest period performs a key function in the decoction mash. At temperatures between about 45°C and 55°C (113-131°F), an enzyme, proteinase, becomes activated and this breaks down high-order proteins that would cause a haze, into simpler, more soluble substances that should not. This particular enzyme is deactivated above 60°C (140°F) and therefore does not operate in the ordinary single-temperature infusion mash.

The boiling of portions of the mash tackles another problem; it gelatinises the undegraded starch that is present in undermodified malts and enables it to be attacked by the enzymes during the mash. The boiling phase of the classic decoction mash is redundant these days. No maltster supplies undermodified malt in this superscientific age. Undermodified malt is also inefficient malt, and brewery accountants tend to wag super-efficient fingers at wasteful brewers. Another problem with the decoction mash is that the regular boiling of a third of the mash will also destroy a third of the available enzymes each time, producing a stepwise reduction in the efficiency of the mash. This can be dangerous with modern malts because they may not be particularly rich in enzymes.

Although the decoction mash is inappropriate for modern malts, the regular boiling is unnecessary, some continental breweries still use it as a matter of tradition, but usually use much simplified versions of its original form. The decoction mash comes in three basic flavours; single, double, and triple-decoction. Temperature and timings can vary somewhat, but the classic triple-decoction mash would proceed as follows:

The grist is mixed into the mash vessel with warm water such that the initial temperature of the mash is 35°C to 40°C (95-104°F). The mash is then allowed to stand for anything from half an hour to two hours depending upon the brewery's preference. Some proteolysis takes place at this temperature, but a major reason for this standing period is to ensure the grist is well mixed and hydrated and that the enzymes are activated. Some German breweries stand the mash at this temperature for several hours to encourage lactic acid bacteria (present naturally on the malt) to lower the pH of the mash, either as an alternative to water treatment or to give the beer a lactic character. The necessary bacteria are most active at these temperatures.

After the standing period has elapsed, about a third of the mash, grain and all, is removed from the mash tun and transferred to the cooker (a saucepan will serve this purpose in home brewing). The temperature of the fraction in the cooker is slowly raised to 65°C (149°F) and held there for about half an hour to allow saccharification to take place. It is then raised to the boil and boiled for about fifteen minutes. This is the first decoction.

The boiled portion of the mash is then added to the main mash and stirred in. This raises the temperature of the main mash to about 50°C (122°F); the optimum temperature for proteolysis. The mash is then allowed to stand for about twenty minutes to half an hour. This is the protein rest period.

After the protein rest period has elapsed, another third of the mash is transferred to the cooker, raised to 65°C (149°F) and held there for about half an hour, and then raised to the boil and then boiled for fifteen minutes. This is the second decoction.

The boiled portion of the mash is then added back to the main mash and stirred in as before. This raises the temperature to about 65°C (149°F); the optimum for saccharification. The mash is allowed to stand for about an hour. During this period starches are being converted to fermentable sugars.

After the standing period has elapsed the third decoction takes place. Again a third of the mash is transferred to the cooker and boiled for fifteen minutes. The boiled portion is added back to the main mash which raises the temperature to about 76°C (169°F). This is the optimum temperature for starch liquefaction, which reduces wort viscosity and aids run-off. It also deactivates the enzymes. The mash is then transferred to another vessel known as a lauter tun, where the sweet wort is run off and the goods sparged in the ordinary manner.

The lauter tun is a separate vessel where the wort is separated from the grain and the grain sparged. This has a false bottom similar to a traditional British mash tun. The Germans were forced to use a separate vessel because the decoction mash involves a good deal of pumping the mash, grain and all, from the mash vessel to the mash cooker and back again. This would obviously be impossible if the main mash vessel had a false bottom holding the grain back, as in British mash tuns. Home brewers do not normally pump their mash around, so they are free to use a mash tun with an integral false bottom should they wish.

The above description refers to the triple-decoction mash, but the triple decoction is not much used these days because, apart from being inappropriate for modern malts, it is inefficient in both time and energy. The 40°C stand does not really achieve much unless cooked cereals are being added, or unless bacterial acidification of the mash is desired. The double decoction process dispenses with this stand. With the double-decoction mash, the grist is mixed in at 50°C (122°F) instead of 40°C (104°F). Two decoctions, or boils, are then employed to raise the temperature, first to 65-67°C (149-121°F) and then to 76°C (169°F) as described above.

The situation can be simplified even further. The 76°C temperature step can also be dispensed with. It is not necessary to raise the temperature before running off and sparging, infusion mash brewers have been running off at normal saccharification temperatures for centuries. This brings us to the single-decoction mash which is by far the most common form of decoction mash employed these days. The single-decoction mash is started at 50°C (122°F), held for twenty minutes or so; raised by decoction to 63-67°C (145-121°F), held for an hour and then sparged in the normal manner with water at 77°C (171°F).

TEMPERATURE-STEPPED INFUSION MASH

The classic decoction mash is, from the technical standpoint, redundant these days because nobody uses undermodified malt, and because the regular boiling of a portion of the mash will progressively destroy a large part of the mash enzymes. Another problem with the decoction mash is that the boiling can cause a glutinous mash that is difficult to run-off and sparge, and requires a traditional type of lauter tun with a broad, shallow grain bed for efficient sparging.

Although the boiling phase of the decoction mash is undesirable, the 50°C (122°F) protein rest period is useful. The barley grown in many countries is often high in nitrogen and the protein rest at 50°C is still necessary when using high nitrogen malts, typical of continental malts, particularly with beers that are adjunct free and expected to be served highly chilled. Lager malt should always be assumed to have a high nitrogen content, and should be given a protein rest period at 50-52°C as a matter of course.

The modern equivalent of the decoction mash is the temperature-stepped infusion mash. Commercial brewers that use a temperature-stepped infusion mash usually have a mash tun that is heated in some way to enable temperature profiling similar to that of a decoction mash to be achieved without the undesirable boiling phase.

Although a number of brewers, particularly home brewers, use complicated regimes when using a temperature-stepped mash, the only two really important temperatures are a protein rest at somewhere around 50°C (122°F) followed by a saccharification rest at somewhere around 65°C (149°F). This dual-temperature mash, entailing just one temperature increase, is fairly straightforward to accomplish at home by merely adding hot water to the mash.

BASIC SINGLE-STEP UPWARD INFUSION MASH

This simple technique is very widely used by home brewers, and is perfectly adequate for any recipe in this book that calls up a decoction or temperature-stepped mash, irrespective of the number of steps actually specified. A temperature stepped mash of some sort is the preferred mash in the home-brew environment because it is much easier to perform than the true decoction mash and there little risk of having problems with a glutinous mash as mentioned above.

Add water at a temperature of about 56°C (133°F) to the empty mash tun, at a rate of about two litres of water per kilogram of grain to be mashed. Allow a few minutes for the temperature of the tun to stabilise and then re-check the temperature and adjust to 55°C (131°F) if necessary. When the temperature is correct, stir in the grain very thoroughly to avoid dry pockets, and then measure the temperature of the resulting mash. The temperature should have fallen to 50-52°C (126-129°F). If the temperature is not correct, adjust by adding hot or cold water as appropriate, and stirring it in. Anywhere between 48°C and 54°C (118-129°F) will do, even wider tolerances can be tolerated, but it is best to aim for 50-52°C (122-126°F). When all is okay, fit the lid to the mash tun and leave to stand for thirty minutes. This is the protein rest period.

When the thirty minute stand is over, slowly and carefully add sufficient boiling water to raise the temperature of the mash to 65-68°C (149-154°F), stirring it in thoroughly. Take your time, there is no rush, add the water in discrete stages, stir well, and allow a bit of time between stages for things to stabilise before taking the thermometer reading. When the temperature is right, fit the lid and leave to stand for 60 minutes. After the 60 minute stand, run off and sparge in the normal manner.

This is shown in tabular form in table 6.1

Table 6.1: single step mash programme
Equivalent to single decoction

Mash-in at:	**50-52°C (122-126°F)**	stand for 30 minutes
Raise to:	**65-67°C (149-153°F)**	stand for 1 hour
Sparge water:	**75-79°C (167-174°F)**	

TWO AND THREE STEP MASH PROGRAMMES

Although the simple temperature stepped mash programme of table 6.1 is perfectly suitable for almost any beer or lager using high nitrogen malt, some home brewers may wish to imitate the double and triple decoction mashes. The following tables show suitable programmes. Although it is possible to invoke a double step mash, as in table 6.2, by the simple expedient of adding hot water, the triple step mashes will almost certainly demand the use of a heated mash tun of some sort.

Table 6.2: double step mash programme
Equivalent to double decoction

Mash-in at:	**50-52°C (122-126°F)**	stand for 30 minutes
Raise to:	**65-67°C (149-153°F)**	stand for 1 hour
Raise to:	**75-77°C (167-171°F)**	and run off
Sparge water:	**77-79°C (171-174°F)**	

Table 6.3: triple step mash programme
Equivalent to triple decoction

Mash-in at:	**38-42°C (100-108°F)**	
Raise to:	**50-52°C (122-126°F)**	stand for 30 minutes
Raise to:	**65-67°C (149-153°F)**	stand for 1 hour
Raise to:	**75-77°C (167-171°F)**	and run off
Sparge water:	**77-79°C (171-174°F)**	

The mash of table 6.3 is suitable for those recipes that add cooked cereals, such as grits, to the mash. There are no such recipes in this book. The cooked cereals should be added while the mash is standing at 40°C, the addition of the hot cereals should raise the temperature fairly close to the 50°C stage.

Table 6.4: triple step mash programme
Alternative to table 6.3

Mash-in at:	52°C (122°F)	stand for 30 minutes
Raise to:	62°C (144°F)	stand for 30 minutes
Raise to:	70°C (158°F)	stand for 30 minutes
Raise to:	76°C (169°F)	and run off
Sparge water:	78°C (172°F)	

Table 6.4 is a typical, widely quoted, mashing regime that imitates the triple-decoction method. Table 6.5 shows the optimum temperatures for the various enzymic reactions which take place during a temperature stepped infusion mash. The actual temperatures employed often vary from the optimums, usually at a point somewhere between two optimums so that two enzymes are working in concert. Not all mashing methods have steps at all of the temperatures shown. Methods vary according to the characteristics desired. Observe that the 60°C, 65°C, and 70°C temperatures are similar to the single temperature infusion mash and the same rules apply.

Table 6.5	Optimum temperatures for mash reactions.
Temp	Comments
40°C (104°F)	A temperature stepped mash is sometimes started at this temperature, particularly if cooked cereals are to be added to the mash which would raise its temperature close to the optimum for proteolysis. Some German brewers stand the mash at this temperature for 24-48 hours to encourage lactic acid bacteria to grow and acidify the mash.
50°C (122°F)	Optimum temperature for the protein rest, where proteolysis and some amylosysis takes place. Most temperature stepped mashes are started at this temperature. It is very tolerant, anywhere between 45°C and 55°C will give satisfactory results. Standing period can be anything from 15 minutes to one hour depending upon quantity of starchy adjuncts in the grist.
60°C (140°F)	Optimum temperature for beta-amylase activity which converts starch into fermentable sugars.A beer mashed entirely at temperatures close to this would be fairly dry and relatively high in alcohol.
65°C (149°F)	Optimum temperature for diastase activity which refers to alpha-amylase and beta-amylase working together synergistically. A beer mashed entirely at this temperature would have a well balanced ratio of fermentable to non-fermentable sugars.
70°C (158°F)	Optimum temperature for alpha-amylase activity which converts starch into non-fermentable dextrins. A beer mashed entirely at a temperature close to this value would be high in body and mouth-feel, but relatively low in alcohol.
76°C (169°F)	Optimum temperature for liquefaction which reduces wort viscosity and aids mash tun run-off. Arrests beta-amylase activity but permits some alpha-amylase activity.
78°C (172°F)	Typical sparge water temperature, same as in ordinary infusion mash.

MASHING EQUIPMENT

Probably the easiest method of mashing, at least for a single or dual-temperature infusion mash, is to mash in a standard brewing bin, insulated with tank insulation or a blanket. There are several variations on the theme.

An inexpensive, commercially made, perforated plastic false bottom, known as Phil's Phalse Bottom, is available which will fit into a standard unmodified brewing bin and instantly convert it into a mash tun that closely resembles the commercial brewer's equivalent. The same combination can be used as a lauter tun if you need to mash in a separate vessel, say using a stove-top stock pot.

Alternatively, you can mash in a standard brewing bin unmodified, and not fitted with a false bottom, and then transfer the mash to a separate vessel, known as a lauter tun, for straining and sparging. See lauter tun, below.

HOME MADE MASH TUN AND FALSE BOTTOM

It is possible to make a mash tun and false bottom from two standard brewing bins, as I did before "phalse bottoms" were available commercially. This uses two fermentation buckets, one inserted inside the other. The inside one has holes drilled in the base to make a false bottom for run off and sparging, and the outside bucket has a tap fitted to enable the wort to be run off at will. During mashing the contraption is lagged with insulation to prevent heat loss. The same device can also serve as a hop-back or a lauter tun. The two bins should be identical, except that the outer bin should have a tap fitted, and the inner bin should not. The inner bin should be equipped with a close fitting lid. The type of bin employed for this application should be of the highly-tapered, bucket-shaped variety, not the tall, narrow type which will not allow the inner bin to be inserted far enough inside the outer one.

The base of the inner bin should be drilled with a matrix of 2mm holes spaced about 10-15mm apart. For a bin with a 280mm (11-inch) base, about 500 or 600 holes drilled symmetrically around the base on a spider web pattern will be sufficient. It is not such a formidable task as it may seem and does not take very long. Stick a sheet of graph paper to the base of the bin as a drilling guide. The outer bin is unmodified apart from having a tap fitted. The tap should be fitted fairly close to the bottom to minimise the amount of wasted space under the false bottom. The tun is assembled by pushing the drilled inner bin down into the outer bin as far as it will go. It should rest upon the outer bin tap-fixing nut.

48

INSULATING HOME-MADE MASH TUNS

During mashing, the tun is insulated by wrapping strips of plastic covered water-tank insulation around the outside of the outer bin. The strips are held in position by stretchy luggage straps in my case, but they could also be held in position by string or adhesive tape. During the mash the lid is fitted to the inner bin and more strips of insulation are laid over the top to reduce the heat loss through the lid. An old blanket would also serve as insulation.

BREWING BIN (OR BOILER) FITTED WITH A GRAIN BAG

If you do not wish to turn your hand to drilling holes in a brewing bin, an alternative is to use a grain-bag in conjunction with your boiler. Any home-brew shop will supply you with a fine-mesh grain-bag. However, grain bags are messy and difficult to use. In addition, the boiler is occupied with mashing duties when it could be better employed elsewhere; heating sparge liquor for instance. However, many home brewers use the grain-bag method, and almost every "masher" learned his craft using one.

INSULATED PICNIC BOX MASH TUN

A mash tun fashioned from an insulated picnic box or cool box was first described by Dave Line in 1974 and is still a fairly common method of mashing. A commercially manufactured version of this is available from home brew shops that has a perforated straining pipe fitted in the bottom, making a false bottom or lauter tun unnecessary.

MASHING USING A FLOATING MASH TUN

Some home brewers mash by floating an unmodified fermentation bin in their brewing boiler. No grain-bag is employed, but a separate vessel is required to separate the grain from the wort. The separate vessel is very similar to a mash tun, only it is called a lauter-tun. The advantage of the floating mash tun is that the water jacket isolates the tun from the source of heat, providing a buffer, enabling very gentle adjustments of temperature to be performed with reduced danger of hot spots destroying the enzymes. This method is particularly useful for temperature stepped mashing, but a large boiler is needed to accommodate a fermentation bin.

STOVE-TOP STOCK-POT MASH TUN

Stove top mashing is another fairly common mashing method that enables temperature adjustments to be made fairly readily. It is particularly useful when a brewer wishes to perform a temperature stepped mash using a large number of steps, where some form of heating will be necessary. A large aluminium or stainless steel stock pot, or a large dixie made from suitable material, stood on the kitchen stove is all that it entails. False bottoms or grain bags are impractical with this method, thus a lauter tun is necessary for separating the wort from the grain.

Temperature adjustments are made by direct heat to the vessel, thus there is the danger of generating hot-spots and destroying valuable enzymes. Apart from destroying enzymes, overheating can cause a thick glutinous, porridge-like mash that is difficult to run off. It is important to apply heat very gently, stirring continuously, when raising the temperature. The rate of rise should not exceed about 1-2°C per minute. Some home brewers make a temperature buffer by suspending or supporting their mash tun in another, shallow vessel filled with water.

LAUTER TUN

Some mash tuns have an integral perforated false bottom which acts as a strainer to separate the grain from the wort during run off and sparging. In some cases, however, a false bottom or a grain bag is impractical during mashing and it is far more convenient to mash in a standard, unmodified vessel of some sort and transfer the mash to a separate vessel for wort separation, run-off and sparging. This separate straining vessel is usually referred to as a lauter tun.

Probably the easiest way of making a lauter tun is to line a standard brewing bin with a nylon grain bag or straining bag. The bag should be big enough to fit the bin snugly against the sides, and it can be held in place by clothes-pegs clipped to the rim. The bin should have a tap fitted and run-off is achieved via this. It may be necessary to keep the bag away from the tap, which could otherwise block it. This can be achieved by shielding the tap with a saucer, saucepan-lid, coffee cup or something of that nature.

Alternatively, Phil's phalse bottom can be used to make a lauter tun and the home made mash tun described above will also serve admirably as a lauter tun.

RUN-OFF AND SPARGING

Whatever type of mash or mash tun employed, the final stage is to run off the sweet wort and sparge the grains. Sparging entails gently spraying hot water, at a temperature of about 77-80°C, over the goods in the mash tun to rinse out any entrapped sugars. The grain is held back in the mash tun or lauter tun by a perforated false bottom, a grain bag or some other straining device. The grain acts as a filter bed and filters the wort bright. Sparging must be performed gently, otherwise the filter bed of grain could crack and allow debris into the wort.

Sparging is usually performed by heating the water in the hot liquor tank to a temperature of 77-80°C (171-176°F) and spraying the water over the grains in a very fine, light spray. Many home brewers simply use a fine watering-can rose attached by a length of polythene tubing to the hot liquor tank, others fill a small indoor plant waterer and use that. A home made static spray ring works well. Proper rotating sparge arms, made specially for home brewing in a variety of sizes, are available from home-brew shops.

If such refinements are unavailable, the simplest method is simply to pour jugfuls of hot water over the grains taking care to ensure that the bed does not break up. This can be achieved by placing a small object in the centre of the mash, perhaps a saucer (something smaller would be better), and pouring the water directly on to this. It will cause the water to splash about all over the place, but greatly reduces the risk of cracking the grain bed.

Run-off and sparging are often performed simultaneously; that is, the tap on the mash tun is turned on to run off the sweet wort at a very slow trickle, and sparging is started at the same time. The specific gravity of the outflow from the tun is monitored and sparging is halted when this falls to below about 1008. Over-sparging should be avoided because it favours the extraction of undesirable substances from the grains which cause off-tastes and hazes and affect head retention, apart from the risk of over diluting the wort.

It must be stressed that sparging is a slow process; it must not be rushed. In commercial breweries the run-off and sparging operation can take two hours or more. If you break up the mash bed and end up with a turbid wort you may end up with a cloudy beer.

Miscellaneous matters

This section deals with those aspects of the brewing process that are fairly standard, irrespective of the type of beer being brewed, and do not justify a chapter to themselves.

WATER TREATMENT

Water treatment for brewing is a very emotive subject and is as fiercely argued and debated by home brewers today as it was by commercial brewers in times past. Unfortunately there is quite a lot of myth, mystery and exaggerated importance surrounding water treatment, particularly in home brewing circles, but there has been as much rubbish written in commercial brewing books about the benefits of water treatment as there has in home brewing books – we have simply carried the tradition on.

One of the biggest myths, that dark beers prefer carbonate water and pale beers prefer gypseous water, simply is not true. What is true, from the scientific perspective at least, is that carbonates are detrimental to beer and sulphates are beneficial, but they are theoretical benefits, mostly only of importance to commercial brewers. In practice it does not seem to make a ha'porth of difference to the majority of home brewed beers, from the flavour perspective, whether the water is treated or not.

It may be true to say that in order to duplicate exactly a particular brewer's beer you may need to duplicate his water supply, but even so, I am sceptical. Any commercial brewer today who treats his water does not do it to match any particular water supply, or even to keep the mineral content of his own water supply consistent, but to move his mash acidity to below about pH 5.6; closer to the theoretical optimum.

Most modern breweries reduce carbonate hardness to below 25 ppm by adding acids, boiling (rarely), or ion exchange and then add sulphates to lower the mash pH to 5.3 or thereabouts. Maximum mash efficiency occurs at pH 5.3, and as efficiency is all the rage these days, 5.3 is what they go for. Some German brewers, who think that they are prohibited from adding minerals to their water, lower the mash pH by encouraging lactic acid bacteria to grow by standing the mash for several hours at 35-40°C before performing the mash proper.

For those brewers that wish to treat their water, I would suggest the simple, basic water treatment given below. It is my standard treatment that I use for all the beers I brew. There is little point in departing from it much, except in exceptional circumstances, because mash reactions are auto buffering. That is, the mash pH moves so far, readily, and then it stops moving and stubbornly sits there, irrespective of how much calcium sulphate is chucked into the water. By this I mean that beyond a certain point a disproportionately large addition of mineral is required to shift the pH a small degree.

BASIC WATER TREATMENT

Put 25 litres of aerated water into your brewing boiler and bring to the boil. When the water comes to the boil, add 12g calcium sulphate (2 heaped teaspoons) and, optionally, 3g common salt (half teaspoon) then boil vigorously for fifteen minutes to half an hour. When the boiling period is complete switch off the heat and wait for the precipitate to settle out. Then add 2g magnesium sulphate (half teaspoon).

The magnesium sulphate is added last because it can retard the precipitation of carbonates. It dissolves easily. I often add it after racking the treated water off the precipitated chalk, but sometimes directly to the mash. It is only used as a yeast co-enzyme and has little effect on mash pH. Mash pH is effected to the greatest extent by the calcium sulphate. The common salt is a matter of taste; indeed, many home brewers do not bother with it.

As mentioned earlier, the mash reactions are auto buffering. The addition or subtraction of the primary minerals will only move mash pH so far and very little more from then on. I am not sure of the reactions that cause this effect, but I suspect that it has something to do with the total alkalinity of the water and the free phosphoric acid in the mash. It is, however, possible to shift the pH of a stubborn mash by the addition of acids. A teaspoonful or two of citric or lactic acid added to the water will help persuade a stubborn mash to move. It should be performed after the water has been boiled to remove carbonate, and preferably after the water has been racked off the chalk precipitate.

Do not fall into the trap and think that the pH of your brewing water and the pH of the resultant mash are equivalent – they are not.

THE BOIL

There is no difference if boiling for an ale or a lager. In general, a good rolling boil for a period of between 60 and 90 minutes is sufficient, boiling a volume as close to the final volume of beer as the boiler can accommodate. The longer the boil the more protein will be precipitated and the longer will be the shelf life of the resulting beer. Long boils also give a better hop utilisation. The hop quantities specified in the recipes are calculated on the specified boil time, usually 90 minutes. The minimum boil period that a home brewer could expect to get away with is 60 minutes, although some Berliner wheat beers have very short boiling periods. Too short a boiling period can give problems with the beer gushing and permit hazes to be formed, whereas excessively long boiling periods can give problems with poor head formation due to too many of the head-forming proteins being precipitated.

Whole hops or hop plugs are the most appropriate to home brewing; the hops settle on the false bottom of the boiler or the hop back and act as a filter bed for trub removal. A good dose of Irish moss, 5-15 grams per 25 litre batch, added about fifteen minutes before the end of the boil, is recommended for pale beers. This will help to precipitate excessive protein and should be used as a matter of course for both ales and lagers as a safeguard against poor quality malt. This may not sound very Reinheitsgebot, but it should be remembered that most German brewers, and other European lager brewers, use kiesleguhr or cellulose filtering for protein removal, a technique not normally available to home brewers, although one British home-brew supplier does market miniature electric sheet-filters that are capable of performing this function.

BOILER

We need to boil large volumes of wort, sometimes in excess of our final volume of beer if we over-sparge a high gravity beer. Malt extract brewers can get away with boiling a smaller volume, but even so, it is desirable to boil a volume of wort as close to our final volume of beer as possible. Kitchen utensils can be pressed into service, particularly if a large four or five gallon dixie or stockpot is available, but in general, ordinary kitchen utensils are impractical and a decent electric boiler is almost essential.

There are two types of purpose-built, polypropylene home-brewing boilers available in the shops, the Ritchie Bruheat, and the Thorne Electrim. Unfortunately neither of them is supplied with a false bottom for the hops to settle on when the boil is complete; suitable commercial false bottoms made specifically for these boilers are available from the shops. Alternatively we can either make our own or construct a separate hop-back vessel, and use that to strain the hops and trub out of the wort. I have invested in a couple of Burco stainless steel catering boilers and I have fabricated a perforated false bottom out of copper sheet.

An alternative to using an integral false bottom in the boiler is to use a separate external vessel as a hop-back. The hops can be allowed to boil freely in the wort and then be transferred to the hop-back when the boil is complete. The trub and hops can then be filtered from the wort in the separate hop-back. The home-made mash-tun or the various lauter tuns described in the chapter on mashing are eminently suited for use as hop-backs providing the materials from which they are constructed can withstand the hot wort.

If a separate vessel is employed as a hop-back, the hot wort must be transferred to this vessel, a hazardous process. Unfortunately the taps fitted to boilers are not large enough to allow the spent hops to pass through, and will block if an attempt is made to use them. The easiest method of transferring the hot wort from the boiler to the hop-back is to bail most of the wort across using a small saucepan. When the volume in the boiler has been reduced to an easily manageable level, tip the remainder into the hop-back -hops and all. Allow half-an-hour to one hour for everything to settle, and then run off the clear wort via the tap.

FERMENTATION — ALES

The vast majority of traditional commercial ales are fermented in open fermentation vessels using a traditional ale yeast, at a temperature of around 16°C (60°F). In commercial brewing, the yeast is usually pitched at about 16°C (60°F) and the temperature is allowed to rise to as high as 20-24°C (68-77°F) by the heat naturally evolved by the action of fermentation. When the maximum temperature is reached, water is pumped through the cooling coils to gradually bring the temperature back down.

In the home brewing environment our volumes are too small to experience this natural temperature rise, and the yeasts supplied to us often will not form a head at 16°C (60°F), so a compromise solution is needed. A temperature band at a typical average of the commercial temperature range seems the best solution. I generally advise maintaining the fermentation temperature for an ale somewhere between 18 and 22°C (64-72°F) as a good compromise.

In order to ensure that the yeast head is rapidly formed, it is usually beneficial to pitch the yeast when the wort temperature is relatively high, between 25-30°C (77-86°F), and allow the temperature to drop to a more appropriate fermentation temperature when the head has formed.

Ales will take about 5-7 days to ferment at the appropriate temperatures.

FERMENTATION — LAGERS

It is not accurate to assume that all lagers are fermented in enclosed fermenters at low temperatures. A number of traditional Pilsner breweries in both the Czech Republic and Bavaria ferment in open oak vessels at relatively warm temperatures. In Michael Jackson's World Guide to Beer there is a photograph of a Czech brewer examining a beer in an open oak fermenter, the beer having a yeast head showing good top-working characteristics. By definition at least, it is only the lagering period that needs to be conducted cold.

Nevertheless, conventional wisdom has it that lager fermentations are started at 7-11°C and allowed to rise naturally to 10-15°C, as indeed most modern mass-market lagers are. As with ale fermentation, in the home brewing environment we need to come to some sort of compromise and I generally recommend fermenting lagers at 10-15°C. Whether you ferment in an open or enclosed fermenter is a matter of personal choice, but a winemaker's five gallon fermenter makes a suitable enclosed fermenter. Alternatively you can simply fit the lid to a standard brewing bucket.

Lagers can take 8-10 days to ferment at the appropriate temperatures.

YEAST SKIMMING

Many home brewing books recommend frequent yeast skimming. I do not go along with this. I do not believe in continually interfering with the ale. The only time that I physically skim yeast is if it is in danger of spilling over the sides of the bin, or if undesirable things are on the surface of it, or if it is in danger of collapsing into the ale at the end of fermentation. The beer should be racked off the yeast into a separate vessel at the end of fermentation.

MATURATION

Most beers benefit from a period of maturation. The stronger the beer, the longer the maturation period should be. Weak beers require a minimum of about three weeks; strong beers, a month or two. Maturation is best performed in a cask, irrespective of whether or not the beer is to be bottled.

Transfer of the beer from fermentation vessel to cask should be effected by means of a siphon tube. Care must be taken to ensure that a minimum amount of air comes into contact with the beer by keeping the outlet end of the tube submerged under the beer being transferred. Take care not to transfer any sediment. Ideally the casks should be filled quite full, but that is difficult to achieve with the equipment currently available to us. The cask should then be stowed away and the ale matured for an appropriate period.

If your cask has a large amount of air space remaining, the air should be expelled by carefully releasing and re-sealing the cask cap after two or three days, and it may be beneficial to add about 50 grams of cane sugar primings at the time of filling to generate conditioning gas rapidly

LAGERING

Lagers are, by definition, lagered for a period at low temperatures. Theoretically, during this lagering period haze-forming proteins are precipitated, yeast sediments, and the beer becomes carbonated. The low temperature suppresses the formation of esters and fusel oils by the yeast, therefore little in the way of flavour modification takes place. These days lagers are not lagered for the long periods of old, and filtering removes the yeast and proteins. Classically, lagering takes place at a temperature of 1-4°C (32.5-34.2°F) for anything between four weeks and six months. The amateur would require a refrigerator capable of holding a cask to achieve this type of lagering.

BOTTLING

All beer destined for bottling should first be matured for a time in the cask. Bottling straight from the fermentation vessel is bad practice and should be avoided. A bottle is a tightly sealed container, and the volatile fusel oil products of fermentation have no way of escape. Even the worst commercial breweries mature their bottled beers in a conditioning tank before bottling. Weak beers will need a week or two in cask, strong beers longer still – perhaps a month; and very strong beers for as long as your patience lasts. The ideal time to bottle is just after the ale has cleared in cask.

The beer should have dropped bright before bottling is attempted. The bottles should be filled by means of a siphon tube that reaches to the bottom of the bottle, and the normal precautions should be taken to ensure that a minimum of air is absorbed. They should be filled leaving about half an inch of space in the neck and the bottles should be stored for a minimum of a month, preferably longer.

Brewing Instructions

EASY BREWING METHOD —

MALT EXTRACT — NO MASH REQUIRED

A number of recipes in this book are suitable for brewing using this simple brewing method. With this method no mash is required; the primary malt is replaced by malt extract and all the ingredients are simply boiled together in the boiler. Any type of malt extract can be used, but an ordinary, pale-coloured, non-diastatic extract is preferred.

A selection of recipes that are suitable are indicated in the beers index by an asterisk (*). The recipes thus marked will specify in a footnote to the main recipe the quantity of malt extract to be used.

PREPARATION

Choose a recipe indicated with a (*) in the beers index. Simply omit the primary malt called for in the recipe and replace it with the quantity of light-coloured malt extract specified in the footnote to the recipe. Ordinary malt extract can be used, the special diastatic type is not necessary.

Make up a yeast starter solution a couple of days before you intend to brew. Stand the container of malt extract in hot water for five or ten minutes prior to brewing in order to soften it.

THE BOIL

Put about 18 litres (4 gallons) of water into the boiler and heat to about 40°C (104°F). Stir in the malt extract and other grains, but not the sugars or hops. The heat source should be turned off while the malt extract is being stirred in to prevent it scorching on the heater before it is properly dissolved, and thereby run the danger of darkening the beer. When the extract is fully dissolved, turn the heat on and bring to the boil. Some people object to boiling the grain on the grounds that it could introduce grainy off-tastes. An alternative is to put the grains into some sort of muslin bag, put into the boiler at about 40°C, allow the boiler to heat up and fish the bag out again before the wort comes to the boil. Add the first batch of hops as soon the wort comes to the boil, and add any sugars or syrups called for about halfway through. A good, vigorous boil for a period of about one-and-a-half hours is required.

About fifteen minutes before the end of the boiling period, the second batch of hops and the Irish moss (if used) are added. Irish moss helps to precipitate haze-forming proteins out of the wort, but there is little benefit to be gained from using it in conjunction with dark beers. When the wort has been boiled for the desired length of time the boiler is switched off and a period is allowed for the trub and hop debris to settle.

If you have a perforated false bottom fitted to your boiler, or if you are using a hop-bag, the wort can be run into a collection vessel, care being taken to ensure that as much debris as possible is left behind in the boiler, filtered by the bed of hops. If you do not have either of these devices then the contents of the boiler should be tipped carefully into a separate hop-back and the filtering done there. If the first runnings are turbid they should be returned to the hop-back for re-filtering.

WORT AERATION

Cool by your own favourite method. After cooling, the wort is adjusted to the correct specific gravity by adding cold water, and then it is aerated. Yeast needs a certain amount of dissolved air to be present in the wort at the start of fermentation in order to multiply and establish itself. The wort boil drives off all the air, so it is important to put some back. This can be achieved by pouring the wort vigorously from one bin to another, generating lots of swirling motion and plenty of mechanical action. Alternatively, simply running the wort slowly from one bin to another, via the tap is all that is required. In this case just one transfer would be sufficient. The wort should be cool before this action is performed because the solubility of oxygen is greater at low temperatures.

FERMENTATION

Ensure that the temperature of the wort is below 30°C before the yeast starter is pitched. The contents of the yeast starter bottle are added to the wort and fermentation will begin. After pitching stand the fermentation vessel in a convenient place where the temperature can be maintained at the proper temperature, usually between about 18°C and 22°C for ales, 10-15°C for lagers. The lid can be fitted to the bin until the yeast head is beginning to form, but should be removed afterwards. When the head has established itself the surface will contain some dark floccules and trub brought up with the yeast. These should be skimmed off, taking care to cause the minimum of disturbance to the rest of the head.

Fermentation methods differ depending upon whether an ale or lager is being brewed. See chapter 7 for more hints on fermentation and on the remainder of the brewing process.

GRAIN BREWING — FULL MASH —
SINGLE INFUSION

All of the recipes in this book are primarily designed for brewing from grain using a full mash. Full mashing is the only brewing method capable of producing exhibition-quality beers, and is the only way of getting close to emulating the commercial beer recipes given within these pages. This section gives basic mashing instructions for the simple infusion mash, traditionally used for ales, the next section give instructions for temperature stepped mashing, appropriate to lager brewing.

PREPARATION

Make up a yeast starter solution a couple of days before you intend to brew. If you treat your water, perform the water treatment the evening before you intend to brew and store it in your cask. This will save about an hour during the brewing session.

All of the malted grains used in the making of ale need to be crushed before they can be successfully mashed. Crushing the malt is a difficult process to perform without the proper equipment. Homebrew shops can supply the stuff already crushed and it should be purchased in this form. Cereal adjuncts such as flaked maize and torrefied barley do not need to be crushed.

MASH LIQUOR

Put 25 litres of treated water into the brewing boiler and heat it to about 77°C. When the liquor is up to temperature run the specified volume of mash liquor into the mash tun. Put the lid on the mash tun and wait a few minutes for the temperature to stabilise. After a few minutes have elapsed check that the temperature of the mash liquor is at strike heat (about 72°C). Adjust the temperature if necessary by adding boiling or cold water.

THE MASH

When you have assured yourself that the temperature of the mash liquor (water) is at strike heat carefully add the grist and stir it into the liquor to form a thick porridge-like mass. This should be done thoroughly to ensure that there are no dry pockets remaining, else an inefficient mash will result.

The act of adding the cold grain to the hot liquor should lower the temperature of the mass to around 67°C; close to the correct mashing temperature. If the mash is not at the proper temperature quickly adjust it to its correct value by adding boiling or cold water and stirring it well into the mash.

The temperature of the mash should be maintained between the limits of 62°C and 69°C for a period of about one-and-a-half hours. Fit the lid, cover it with some insulation, and leave it to stand for the appropriate mashing period. Monitor the temperature periodically and if the temperature falls too low, correct it by adding boiling water and stirring it well in. This should not be necessary if the mash tun is properly insulated.

While the mash is in progress ensure that there is sufficient water in the boiler for sparging, and set the boiler to maintain the sparge liquor at a temperature of 77-80°C.

RUNNING-OFF

After the mash has stood for the specified length of time, usually about one-and-a-half hours, carefully open the tap on the mash tun and allow the sweet wort to run slowly into a collection vessel. Take care to ensure that the flow is not so fast that the grain beds down hard and blocks. The flow should be very low indeed. The grain should act as a filter-bed and filter the wort bright. The first runnings may be turbid, and these should be returned carefully to the mash tun until it runs bright.

SPARGING

While the wort is running off, sparging can begin. This means rinsing the grains with hot water maintained at a temperature of 77-80°C. This rinses out the sugars which are trapped in the grains.

Ideally, the sparge should be a light spray, care being taken to ensure that the mash bed does not crack. Sparging should be performed slowly and carefully! Monitor the gravity of the spargings and stop sparging when this falls to below about 1008 or when sufficient wort has been collected. It is best not to drain the mash bed completely, but to supply sufficient sparge liquor to balance the out-flow from the mash-tun and keep the mash bed floating.

THE BOIL

Once the wort has been collected the boiler should be topped up with water to a volume as near to the final volume as can be achieved, remembering to leave sufficient headroom to accommodate the foam produced during boiling. The boil is then begun.

Add the first batch of hops as soon the wort comes to the boil, and add any sugars or syrups called for about halfway through. A good, vigorous boil for a period of about one-and-a-half hours is required.

About fifteen minutes before the end of the boiling period, the second batch of hops and the Irish moss (if used) are added. Irish moss helps to precipitate haze-forming proteins out of the wort, but there is little benefit to be gained from using it in conjunction with dark beers. When the wort has been boiled for the desired length of time the boiler is switched off and a period is allowed for the trub and hop debris to settle.

If you have a perforated false bottom fitted to your boiler, or if you are using a hop-bag, the wort can be run directly into a collection vessel, care being taken to ensure that as much debris as possible is left behind in the boiler, filtered by the bed of hops. If you are not using either of these devices then the contents of the boiler should be tipped carefully, or bailed into a separate hop-back and the filtering effected there. If the first runnings are turbid they should be returned to the hop-back for re-filtering.

WORT AERATION

Cool by your own favourite method. After cooling, the wort is adjusted to the correct specific gravity by adding cold water, and then it is aerated.

Yeast needs a certain amount of dissolved air to be present in the wort at the start of fermentation in order to multiply and establish itself. The wort boil drives off all the air, so it is important to put some back. This can be achieved by pouring the wort vigorously from one bin to another, generating lots of swirling motion and plenty of mechanical action. Alternatively simply running the wort slowly from one bin to another, via the tap is all that is required. In this case just one transfer would be sufficient. The wort should be cool before this action is performed because the solubility of oxygen is greater at low temperatures.

FERMENTATION

Ensure that the temperature of the wort is below 30°C before the yeast starter is pitched. The contents of the yeast starter bottle is added to the wort and fermentation will begin. After pitching stand the fermentation vessel in a convenient place where the temperature can be maintained at the proper temperature, usually between about 18°C and 22°C for ales. The lid can be fitted to the bin until the yeast head is beginning to form, but should be removed afterwards. When the head has established itself the surface will contain some dark floccules and trub brought up with the yeast. These should be skimmed off, taking care to cause the minimum of disturbance to the rest of the head.

Fermentation methods differ depending upon whether an ale or lager is being brewed. See chapter 7 for more hints on fermentation and on the remainder of the brewing process.

GRAIN BREWING — FULL MASH —
BASIC TEMPERATURE-STEPPED MASH

This simple temperature stepped mash is perfectly adequate for any of the lager-type recipes in this book.

PREPARATION

Make up a yeast starter solution a couple of days before you intend to brew. If you treat your water, perform the water treatment the evening before you intend to brew and store it in your cask. This will save about an hour during the brewing session.

All of the malted grains used in the making of ale need to be crushed before they can be successfully mashed. Crushing the malt is a difficult process to perform without the proper equipment. Home-brew shops can supply the stuff already crushed and it should be purchased in this form. Cereal adjuncts such as flaked maize and tor-refied barley do not need to be crushed.

THE MASH

Add water at a temperature of about 58°C (136°F) to the mash tun, at a rate of about two litres of water per kilogram of grain to be mashed. Allow a few minutes for the temperature of the tun to stabilise and then re-check the temperature and adjust to 55°C (131°F) if necessary.

When the temperature is correct, stir in the grain very thoroughly to avoid dry pockets, and then measure the temperature of the resulting mash. The temperature should have fallen to 50-52°C (126-129°F). If the temperature is not correct, adjust by adding hot or cold water as appropriate, and stirring it in. Anywhere between 48°C and 54°C (118-129°F) will do, even wider tolerances can be tolerated, but it is best to aim for 50-52°C (122-126°F). When all is well, fit the lid to the mash tun and leave to stand for thirty minutes. This is the protein rest period.

When the thirty minute stand is over, slowly and carefully add sufficient boiling water to raise the temperature of the mash to 65-68°C (149-154°F), stirring it in thoroughly. Take your time, there is no rush, add the water in discrete stages, stir well, and allow a bit of time between stages for things to stabilise before taking the thermometer reading. When the temperature is right, fit the lid and leave to stand for 60 minutes. Monitor the temperature periodically and if the temperature falls too low correct it by adding boiling water and stirring it well in. This should not be necessary if the mash tun is properly insulated.

While the mash is in progress ensure that there is sufficient water in the boiler for sparging, and set the boiler to maintain the sparge liquor at a temperature of 77-80°C.

RUNNING-OFF

After the mash has stood for the specified length of time, usually about one-and-a-half hours, carefully open the tap on the mash tun and allow the sweet wort to run slowly into a collection vessel. Take care to ensure that the flow is not so fast that the grain beds down hard and blocks. The flow should be very low indeed. The grain should act as a filter-bed and filter the wort bright. The first runnings may be turbid, and these should be returned carefully to the mash tun until it runs bright.

SPARGING

While the wort is running off, sparging can begin. This means rinsing the grains with hot water maintained at a temperature of 77-80°C. This rinses out the sugars which are trapped in the grains.

Ideally, the sparge should be a light spray, care being taken to ensure that the mash bed does not crack. Sparging should be performed slowly and carefully! Monitor the gravity of the spargings and stop sparging when this falls to below about 1008 or when sufficient wort has been collected. It is best not to drain the mash bed completely, but to supply sufficient sparge liquor to balance the out-flow from the mash-tun and keep the mash bed floating.

THE BOIL

Once the wort has been collected the boiler should be topped up with water to a volume as near to the final volume as can be achieved, remembering to leave sufficient headroom to accommodate the foam produced during boiling. The boil is then begun.

Add the first batch of hops as soon the wort comes to the boil, and add any sugars or syrups called for about halfway through. A good, vigorous boil for a period of about one-and-a-half hours is required.

About fifteen minutes before the end of the boiling period, the second batch of hops and the Irish moss (if used) are added. Irish moss helps to precipitate haze-forming proteins out of the wort, but there is little benefit to be gained from using it in conjunction with dark beers. When the wort has been boiled for the desired length of time the boiler is switched off and a period is allowed for the trub and hop debris to settle.

If you have a perforated false bottom fitted to your boiler, or if you are using a hop-bag, the wort can be run directly into a collection vessel, care being taken to ensure that as much debris as possible is left behind in the boiler, filtered by the bed of hops. If you are not using either of these devices then the contents of the boiler should be tipped carefully, or bailed into a separate hop-back and the filtering carried out there. If the first runnings are turbid they should be returned to the hop-back for re-filtering.

WORT AERATION

Cool by your own favourite method. After cooling, the wort is adjusted to the correct specific gravity by adding cold water, and then it is aerated.

Yeast needs a certain amount of dissolved air to be present in the wort at the start of fermentation in order to multiply and establish itself. The wort boil drives off all the air, so it is important to put some back. This can be achieved by pouring the wort vigorously from one bin to another, generating lots of swirling motion and plenty of mechanical action. Alternatively simply running the wort slowly from one bin to another, via the tap is all that is required. In this case just one transfer would be sufficient. The wort should be cool before this action is performed because the solubility of oxygen is greater at low temperatures.

FERMENTATION

Ensure that the temperature of the wort is below 30°C before the yeast starter is pitched. The contents of the yeast starter bottle is added to the wort and fermentation will begin. After pitching stand the fermentation vessel in a convenient place where the temperature can be maintained at the proper temperature, usually between about 18°C and 22°C for ales. The lid can be fitted to the bin until the yeast head is beginning to form, but should be removed afterwards. When the head has established itself the surface will contain some dark floccules and trub brought up with the yeast. These should be skimmed off, taking care to cause the minimum of disturbance to the rest of the head.

Fermentation methods differ depending upon whether an ale or lager is being brewed. See chapter 7 for more hints on fermentation and on the remainder of the brewing process.

About the recipes

All the recipes are designed around an 80 per cent mash efficiency and a volume 5 per cent greater than the published final volume of beer to compensate for fermentation losses. The recipes given will not necessarily be exact replicas of the commercial brewery's recipe because, in many cases, although the ingredients were known, the exact ratios were not and these had to be derived empirically. In other cases the recipes have been reformulated to use easily available ingredients. Where caramel is used in the commercial beer to provide colour, this has been omitted and darker malts have been added to balance the colour. Where torrefied cereals or grits are used by the commercial brewer, these have been replaced by flaked cereals. Ordinary domestic cane sugar has been substituted where the commercial brewer uses invert sugar, candy sugar, or other brewing syrups.

Although an attempt has been made to classify the beers into appropriate beer styles, it has not always been possible to strictly categorise some beers because they overlap several styles. Some beer styles, it would seem, were invented by beer writers to give them something to write about and there exists no real or clear definition.

ORIGINAL GRAVITY

The original gravity given in the recipes is that which is published by the brewery concerned. It is given in both s.g. and degrees Plato.

INGREDIENTS

Ingredients are provided for final volumes of 25 litres, 23 litres, 5 UK gallons and 5 US gallons. The 23 litres and 5 UK gallons columns are virtually equivalent and can be used interchangeably, the other columns are not. For the gallon columns the quantities are given in pounds or ounces as appropriate. Where quantities are given in pounds, they are given in pounds and decimal fractions of a pound, not pounds and ounces: 6.5 lbs = 6½ lbs or 6lb 8oz.

Some of the recipes have been reformulated to use easily available ingredients. All of the ingredients specified, with the exception of whisky malt and bacteria cultures, were available through the homebrew trades of Britain and America at the time of writing. However, in some cases only one wholesaler supplies them.

BREWING METHOD AND MASH SCHEDULE

The brewing method and mash schedule given in the recipes attempt to emulate the type of mashing system that the brewery claims to use. If the brewery uses a triple decoction mash, then the mash method and temperatures given attempt to emulate that, so the home brewer can try to duplicate it if he wishes. In those cases where a complex multi-temperature mash or double or triple decoction is specified, the simple dual-temperature mash given in chapter 10 is perfectly adequate. In many cases perfectly acceptable results would be achieved from a single-temperature infusion mash.

BOIL TIME

This has been standardised at 90 minutes unless the actual boil time for the commercial beer is known. A shorter, 60 minute, boil would probably be perfectly adequate, but it would be unwise to boil for any shorter period than that. The hop bitterness has been calculated on the specified boil time, but most of the hop bitterness has been extracted by 60 minutes in any case.

RACKING GRAVITY

This is provided to give some idea of how far the beer will ferment. It gives the approximate gravity at which active fermentation should abate, and at which time the beer should be transferred to a cask. However, it is only an approximate, calculated figure; far too many things affect this for it to be given with any accuracy. Use your own experience to determine when primary fermentation is over.

ALCOHOL CONTENT

This is given as alcohol by volume (abv) to suit European brewers and by weight (abw) to suit American brewers. This is not the commercial brewers published alcohol content, but a computed figure that reflects the home-brew version of the beer. In most cases, however, the computed version matches the commercial brewer's published specification smack on.

BITTERNESS

In EBUs, same as IBUs, and the international standard method of assessing the bitterness of beers. The bitterness of most of the commercial beers specified in this book are known, and the bitterness figures were used to calculate the appropriate quantity of hops to use.

COLOUR

Colour of the beer is given in EBCs as a guide for those that care about such things. The American SRM method is approximately half the EBC value, but not directly equivalent. It seems that a world standard method of assessing beer colour is being introduced in the near future, so there are likely to be some changes anyway.

MALT EXTRACT VERSIONS

Malt extract versions of some of the beers are given so that malt extract brewers can have a go at producing continental style beers. It would be more difficult to flavour match the commercial beer using malt extract, but I make no guarantees about flavour matching even with fully mashed beers anyway. Nevertheless, the beers produced will still be high quality beers, true to style.

Those beers that have a malt extract version provided will have a footnote in the recipe that gives the appropriate quantity of malt extract to be used. As the main recipes have four columns for four different volumes of beer, the footnote also contains four quantities of malt extract: for 25 litres, 23 litres, 5 UK gallons and 5 US gallons. The malt extract recipes have been designed to use ordinary pale-coloured, non-diastatic, malt extract syrup.

Ales

ALES, ALTS, BIÈRES DE GARDE, KÖLSCH, TRAPPIST

The beers in this section are members of the ale family, the world's oldest beer style using a method known as top fermentation or more accurately warm fermentation. Today more than 90 per cent of beer in the world is lager, yet interest in ale is growing as the style offers such a rich diversity of aromas and flavours. Working at warm temperatures, ale yeasts create fruity esters that a lager brewer seeks to avoid with cold conditioning. The most famous ales are those from Britain. While lager has made substantial inroads into the British market, ale has never become a sideline and in its finest form, cask conditioned 'real ale', has become a cult drink. Pale ale was a development of the industrial revolution of the 19th century that made it possible for the first time to make pale malt on a substantial commercial basis. Pale ales were brewed first for the colonial trade – hence the name India Pale Ale – but became popular in the home market once they were made available. While pale ale did not replace mild in popularity until the 1950s, it was regarded as the finest of the ale family as a result of the way in which earthy, peppery fertilised English hops were able to express themselves in a sublime balance with sweet malt. Scottish versions of pale ale tend to be a rich, deep copper colour as a result of the use of dark malt and dashes of roasted grain, while hops are used more sparingly as they do not grow in Scotland. Mild ale, once an important constituent of the early porters and stouts, has declined in step with Britain's retreat from industrialisation. A beer that once refreshed millions of blue-collar workers from factories and mines is now confined to a few pockets of the country. The use of dark malts – crystal, amber and chocolate – produces rich and complex flavours while hop rates tend to be low.

Germany has ales, too. Alt means 'old' and the style is confined mainly to the Düsseldorf area, though it has spread across the border into the Netherlands and south into Austria. Alt is a copper-coloured beer due to the use of Vienna, crystal or roasted malts. It has gently fruity/nutty aromas and flavour balanced by good, perfumy hop. By contrast, the Kölsch beers of neighbouring Cologne are a burnished gold in colour and have a restrained hop bitterness. The aim of the brewer is to produce a rich, quenching yet malt-accented beer. The style is held in such high regard that it is protected by government ordinance and cannot be produced outside of the city.

France's ales have been hidden from view for decades and are only now receiving recognition and approval outside their region of production, the Nord-Pas de Calais that shares a border with Belgium with considerable cross-border influences. Bière de garde – 'keeping beer' – has close links with the saisons of French-speaking Belgium. They were originally rural ales, brewed by farmers for their families and workers, and stored in order to provide refreshment during the summer months when brewing was impossible. Although there are pale versions of the style, they tend to be copper or bronze coloured in general, using dark malts, and are generously hopped.

The Trappist ales of Belgium and the Netherlands have emerged from obscurity in recent years as beer lovers have unearthed the profusion of beer styles in that remarkable country. When monks of the Trappist sect were driven from their home in La Trappe in Normandy during the French revolution, they settled in the Low Countries. They could no longer make liqueurs from wine so turned instead to brewing strong ales, using the produce of the surrounding fields. Their ales are an important element of their simple, vegetarian diets, fulfilling a similar function to the 'liquid bread' Bocks of Germany. They range from the pale, orange-yellow colour of Orval to the burnished tawny hues of Chimay and Rochefort. Special yeast cultures and dark malts give complex aromas and flavours of fruit and spices while English and European hops add earthy, peppery and citric character.

ABBAYE NOTRE-DAME
ORVAL

Belgian Trappist beer. Intense peppery aroma. Bitter gooseberry fruit in the mouth, deep dry finish with enormous bitter fruit and hop character. From Brasserie Abbaye Notre-Dame, Orval, Belgium.

ORIGINAL GRAVITY	1055	13.5° Plato	

	25 litres	23 litres	5 UK gals	5 US gals
Pale malt	3,400 gm	3,150 gm	6.8 lb	5.65 lb
Vienna malt	1,150 gm	1,050 gm	2.25 lb	1.9 lb
Caramunich malt	740 gm	680 gm	1.45 lb	1.2 lb
White sucrose	560 gm	520 gm	1.1 lb	15.0 oz

START OF BOIL

Styrian Golding hops	45 gm	40 gm	1.4 oz	1.15 oz
Hallertau hops	30 gm	25 gm	.9 oz	.75 oz

LAST 15 MINUTES OF BOIL

East Kent Golding hops	15 gm	15 gm	.55 oz	.45 oz
Irish moss	10 gm	10 gm	.35 oz	.30 oz

BREWING METHOD
Single-infusion mash; top-fermenting yeast

MASH SCHEDULE	67°C - 90 minutes (152°F)	
BOIL TIME	90 minutes	
RACKING GRAVITY	1009	2.1° Plato
ALCOHOL CONTENT	6.2% by volume	4.9% by weight
BITTERNESS	40 EBU	
COLOUR	25 EBC	

Add the sugar about half way through the boil, the exact timing is unimportant. Mature in cask for six weeks at 16°C (60°F). Dry hop the cask with a few cones of East Kent Goldings at the time of filling. Bottle after six weeks and mature in bottle for a minimum of two months. Orval prime their bottles with cane sugar and add a second, bottom working, yeast for bottle conditioning. Commercial Orval is available unpasteurised, so it should be fairly straightforward to culture the bottling yeast, but an ordinary "real ale" yeast will provide good results. Mature in cask for six weeks at 15-18°C (59-64°F) before bottling, followed by two months in bottle before sampling.

BASS
DRAUGHT BASS

English cask-conditioned ale. Complex aroma of hop resin, butterscotch and pronounced sulphur. Multi-layered mouthfeel, pronounced maltiness offset by delicate hop, long polished finished with apple notes.

ORIGINAL GRAVITY   1043   10.7° Plato

	25 litres	23 litres	5 UK gals	5 US gals
Halcyon pale malt	4,550 gm	4,200 gm	9.1 lb	7.55 lb
Crystal malt	240 gm	220 gm	7.7 oz	6.4 oz

START OF BOIL

Challenger hops	25 gm	25 gm	.85 oz	.7 oz
Northdown hops (seeded)	25 gm	20 gm	.85 oz	.7 oz

LAST 15 MINUTES OF BOIL

Irish moss	10 gm	10 gm	.35 oz	.30 oz

BREWING METHOD
Single-infusion mash; top-working yeast

MASH SCHEDULE	66°C - 90 minutes (151°F)	
BOIL TIME	90 minutes	
RACKING GRAVITY	1010	2.4° Plato
ALCOHOL CONTENT	4.5% by volume	3.5% by weight
BITTERNESS	30 EBU	
COLOUR	18 EBC	

Bass Export Pale Ale is brewed to 1048 to meet legislation in some countries and certain states in America, multiply all the ingredient quantities by 1.12 to brew a 1048 version. The Bass yeast strain is a two strain yeast. Ferment at 18-22°C, condition in cask for three to four weeks before sampling.

MALT EXTRACT VERSION:
Replace the pale malt with the appropriate quantity of pale coloured malt extract syrup and brew using the instructions given in chapter 8. 25l = 3,500 gm: 23l = 3,200 gm: 5UK = 7 lb: 5US = 5.8 lb

BASS
WORTHINGTON WHITE SHIELD

English bottle-conditioned ale. Spices, peppery hop, light fruit and sulphury notes. Malt and spice in the mouth, deep nutty finish with strong hop character and light apple fruit notes.

ORIGINAL GRAVITY 1051   12.6° Plato

	25 litres	23 litres	5 UK gals	5 US gals
Halcyon pale malt	5,320 gm	4,890 gm	10.6 lb	8.85 lb
Crystal malt	370 gm	340 gm	11.8 oz	9.9 oz
START OF BOIL				
Challenger hops	30 gm	30 gm	.95 oz	.8 oz
Northdown hops (seeded)	30 gm	25 gm	.9 oz	.75 oz
LAST 15 MINUTES OF BOIL				
Irish moss	10 gm	10 gm	.35 oz	.30 oz

BREWING METHOD
Single-infusion mash; top-fermenting yeast

MASH SCHEDULE	66°C - 90 minutes (151°F)	
BOIL TIME	90 minutes	
RACKING GRAVITY	1011	2.8° Plato
ALCOHOL CONTENT	5.3% by volume	4.2% by weight
BITTERNESS	35 EBU	
COLOUR: 25 EBC		

White Shield is fermented using Bass's standard two-strain yeast. After fermentation it is matured in conditioning tanks for a few weeks and then filtered, primed, inoculated with a different yeast strain and bottled. It is bottle conditioned at 13-15°C for two to three weeks.

MALT EXTRACT VERSION:
Replace the pale malt with the appropriate quantity of pale coloured malt extract syrup and brew using the instructions given in chapter 8.
25l = 4,100 gm: 23l = 3,750 gm: 5UK = 8.2 lb: 5US = 6.8 lb

BELHAVEN
EXPORT ALE

Scottish export ale. Rich fruit, malt and toffee aromas. Light fruit and hop in the mouth, deep complex finish with malt, some fruit and developing hop notes.

ORIGINAL GRAVITY 1044.0 10.9° Plato

	25 litres	**23 litres**	**5 UK gals**	**5 US gals**
Pale malt	3,800 gm	3,500 gm	7.6 lb	6.3 lb
Crystal malt	720 gm	660 gm	1.4 lb	1.2 lb
Black malt	48 gm	44 gm	1.5 oz	1.3 oz
White sucrose	240 gm	220 gm	7.7 oz	6.4 oz

START OF BOIL

Golding hops	22 gm	21 gm	.7 oz	.6 oz
Fuggle hops	26 gm	24 gm	.9 oz	.7 oz
Whitbread Golding hops	19 gm	18 gm	.6 oz	.5 oz

LAST 15 MINUTES OF BOIL

Irish moss	10 gm	10 gm	.35 oz	.30 oz

BREWING METHOD
Single-infusion mash; top-fermenting yeast

MASH SCHEDULE	66°C - 90 minutes (151°F)	
BOIL TIME	90 minutes	
RACKING GRAVITY	1010	2.4° Plato
ALCOHOL CONTENT	4.6% by volume	3.6% by weight
BITTERNESS	28 EBU	
COLOUR	60 EBC	

MALT EXTRACT VERSION:
Replace the pale malt with the appropriate quantity of pale coloured malt extract syrup and brew using the instructions given in chapter 8. 25l = 2,900 gm: 23l = 2,700 gm: 5UK = 5.8 lb: 5US = 4.9 lb

CALEDONIAN
EDINBURGH STRONG ALE

Scottish ale. Assault of hop resin, malt, fruit and nut with apple hints. Mouth-filling grain and hop, intense, dry vinous finish.

ORIGINAL GRAVITY	1078		18.7° Plato	

	25 litres	23 litres	5 UK gals	5 US gals
Pale malt	7,550 gm	6,950 gm	15.1 lb	12.6 lb
Amber malt	435 gm	400 gm	13.87 oz	11.56 oz
Crystal malt	360 gm	330 gm	11.46 oz	9.56 oz
Wheat malt	380 gm	350 gm	12.19 oz	10.16 oz

START OF BOIL

Golding hops	60 gm	55 gm	1.90 oz	1.59 oz
Fuggle hops	105 gm	95 gm	3.35 oz	2.8 oz

LAST 15 MINUTES OF BOIL

Irish moss	10 gm	10 gm	.35 oz	.30 oz

BREWING METHOD
Single-infusion mash; top-fermenting yeast

MASH SCHEDULE	66°C - 90 minutes (151°F)	
BOIL TIME	90 minutes	
RACKING GRAVITY	1018	4.3° Plato
ALCOHOL CONTENT	8.1% by volume	6.3% by weight
BITTERNESS	60 EBU	
COLOUR	35 EBC	

CHIMAY
CHIMAY RED

Belgian Trappist beer. The most famous of the Trappist beers outside of Belgium. Soft creamy vanilla aroma with good prickle of hops. Gentle fruit and malt in the mouth, creamy finish with underlying bitter hop notes. From the Abbaye de Notre-Dame, Forges, Belgium.

ORIGINAL GRAVITY	1063	15.3° Plato

	25 litres	23 litres	5 UK gals	5 US gals
Pale malt	5,720 gm	5,270 gm	11.45 lb	9.55 lb
Amber malt	340 gm	310 gm	10.7 oz	9.0 oz
Chocolate malt	100 gm	90 gm	3.1 oz	2.0 oz
White sucrose	550 gm	500 gm	1.05 lb	.9 lb
START OF BOIL				
Hallertau hops	25 gm	20 gm	.8 oz	.7 oz
Tettnang hops	35 gm	30 gm	1.1 oz	.9 oz
LAST 15 MINUTES OF BOIL				
Hallertau hops	15 gm	15 gm	.5 oz	.45 oz
Irish moss	10 gm	10 gm	.35 oz	.30 oz

BREWING METHOD
Single-infusion mash; top-fermenting yeast

MASH SCHEDULE	67°C - 90 minutes (152°F)	
BOIL TIME	90 minutes	
RACKING GRAVITY	1011	2.6° Plato
ALCOHOL CONTENT	7.0% by volume	5.5% by weight
BITTERNESS	28 EBU	
COLOUR: 45 EBC		

This recipe is very much a calculated guess; Chimay are quite secretive about their ingredients and methods. Nevertheless, brewing trials indicate that this recipe is pretty close. Some references suggest that no sugar is used in Chimay beers, but the percentage alcohol quoted by the brewery is fairly high for an all malt beer of OG 1063. The small amount (8%) of sugar is included to make OGs and ABVs match. Add the sugar about half way through the boil, the exact timing is unimportant. Many of the characteristics of Chimay are imparted by their unique yeast. Chimay is bottle-conditioned and unpasteurised, so the yeast can be cultured from any bottle. See Chimay White on the next page.

CHIMAY
CHIMAY WHITE

Belgian Trappist beer .The bigger and paler brother of Chimay Red (previous page). Peppery hop and grain aroma. Fruit in the mouth, light dry finish with hop and sultana fruit notes. From the Abbaye de Notre-Dame, Forges, Belgium.

ORIGINAL GRAVITY   1071   17.2° Plato

	25 litres	23 litres	5 UK gals	5 US gals
Pale malt	6,350 gm	5,820 gm	12.65 lb	10.55 lb
Amber malt	325 gm	300 gm	11.3 oz	8.6 oz
Crystal malt	225 gm	210 gm	7.3 oz	6.1 oz
White sucrose	650 gm	600 gm	1.3 lb	1.05 lb

START OF BOIL

	25 litres	23 litres	5 UK gals	5 US gals
Hallertau hops	25 gm	25 gm	.8 oz	.7 oz
Tettnang hops	35 gm	30 gm	1.1 oz	1.0 oz

LAST 15 MINUTES OF BOIL

	25 litres	23 litres	5 UK gals	5 US gals
Hallertau hops	15 gm	15 gm	.55 oz	.45 oz
Irish moss	10 gm	10 gm	.35 oz	.30 oz

BREWING METHOD
Single-infusion mash; top-fermenting yeast

MASH SCHEDULE	67°C - 90 minutes (152°F)
BOIL TIME	90 minutes
RACKING GRAVITY	1012 2.8° Plato
ALCOHOL CONTENT	8.0% by volume 6.3% by weight
BITTERNESS	30 EBU
COLOUR	25 EBC

This recipe is very much a calculated guess; Chimay are quite secretive about their ingredients and methods. Nevertheless, brewing trials indicate that this recipe is pretty close. Some references suggest that no sugar is used in Chimay beers, but the percentage alcohol quoted by the brewery is fairly high for an all malt beer of OG 1071. The small amount (8%) of sugar is included to make OGs and ABVs match. Add the sugar about half way through the boil, the exact timing is unimportant. Many of the characteristics of Chimay are imparted by their unique yeast. Commercial Chimay is bottle-conditioned and unpasteurised, so the genuine yeast can be cultured from any bottle; it's pretty vigorous stuff.

CORNISH BREWERY
CHURCHILL AMBER BEER

English bottled pale ale. Peppery hop aroma and pear-drop fruitiness. Malt in the mouth, rich blackcurrant fruit finish with good hop notes.

ORIGINAL GRAVITY	1050	12.3° Plato

	25 litres	23 litres	5 UK gals	5 US gals
Pale malt	3,770 gm	3,470 gm	7.55 lb	6.3 lb
Amber malt	510 gm	475 gm	1.0 lb	13.7 oz
Crystal malt	470 gm	430 gm	15.0 oz	12.5 oz
White sucrose	540 gm	500 gm	1.05 lb	14.5 oz

START OF BOIL

Challenger hops	25 gm	25 gm	.9 oz	.7 oz
Golding hops	40 gm	35 gm	1.3 oz	1.1 oz

LAST 15 MINUTES OF BOIL

Irish moss	10 gm	10 gm	.35 oz	.30 oz

BREWING METHOD
Single-infusion mash; top-working yeast

MASH SCHEDULE	66°C - 90 minutes (151°F)	
BOIL TIME	90 minutes	
RACKING GRAVITY	1008	1.9° Plato
ALCOHOL CONTENT	5.7% by volume	4.5% by weight
BITTERNESS	32 EBU	
COLOUR	35 EBC	

This is a British export beer, not found in the UK. Ferment at 18-22°C, mature in cask for four weeks before bottling. Priming sugar is not necessary when bottling, but can be used if desired. Bottle condition for two weeks if priming sugar is used, six weeks if it is not used.

COURAGE
BULLDOG STRONG ALE

English bottled pale ale. Rich malt, peppery hop and some orange fruit on the nose. Pronounced hop on the tongue, long complex finish, bitter-sweet becoming dry with fruit notes.

ORIGINAL GRAVITY	1068.0	16.5° Plato	

	25 litres	23 litres	5 UK gals	5 US gals
Pale malt	6,100 gm	5,600 gm	12.1 lb	10.1 lb
Crystal malt	350 gm	300 gm	11.4 oz	9.5 oz
White sucrose	750 gm	700 gm	1.45 lb	1.2 lb

START OF BOIL

	25 litres	23 litres	5 UK gals	5 US gals
Challenger hops	70 gm	65 gm	2.3 oz	1.9 oz

LAST 15 MINUTES OF BOIL

	25 litres	23 litres	5 UK gals	5 US gals
Golding hops	20 gm	20 gm	.7 oz	.6 oz
Irish moss	10 gm	10 gm	.35 oz	.30 oz

BREWING METHOD
Single-infusion mash; top-fermenting yeast

MASH SCHEDULE	66°C - 90 minutes (151°F)	
BOIL TIME	90 minutes	
RACKING GRAVITY	1011	2.6° Plato
ALCOHOL CONTENT	7.7% by volume	6.1% by weight
BITTERNESS	42 EBU	
COLOUR	26 EBC	

This beer is dry hopped with Styrian Goldings. Add three or four cones of Styrians to the maturation cask and leave for at least two weeks before bottling. Alternatively, soak about 15 grams of hops for half an hour in the hot wort at the end of the boil. The commercial version of this beer is pasteurised in bottle.

MALT EXTRACT VERSION:
Replace the pale malt with the appropriate quantity of pale coloured malt extract syrup and brew using the instructions given in chapter 8.
25l = 4,700 gm: 23l = 4,300 gm: 5UK = 9.4 lb: 5US = 7.8 lb

DE DOLLE
OERBIER

Belgian dark ale. Vinous, sultana aroma with peppery Goldings hop notes. Massive fruit in the mouth with a deep bitter-sweet sherry finish.

ORIGINAL GRAVITY	1065	15.8° Plato

	25 litres	23 litres	5 UK gals	5 US gals
Munich malt (light)	5,160 gm	4,750 gm	10.3 lb	8.6 lb
Amber malt	680 gm	620 gm	1.35 lb	1.1 lb
Chocolate malt	130 gm	120 gm	4.2 oz	3.5 oz
White sucrose	810 gm	750 gm	1.6 lb	1.35 lb
START OF BOIL				
Golding hops	30 gm	30 gm	1.0 oz	.9 oz
Saaz hops	30 gm	30 gm	1.0 oz	.8 oz
LAST 15 MINUTES OF BOIL				
Irish moss	10 gm	10 gm	.35 oz	.30 oz

BREWING METHOD
Single-infusion mash; top-fermenting yeast

MASH SCHEDULE	66°C - 90 minutes (151°F)	
BOIL TIME	90 minutes	
RACKING GRAVITY	1010	2.4° Plato
ALCOHOL CONTENT	7.4% by volume	5.8% by weight
BITTERNESS	26 EBU	
COLOUR	76 EBC	

Ferment at 18-22°C, mature in cask for two to four weeks before bottling. Do not prime bottles, leave for 6-8 weeks in bottle at 13°C (55°F) before sampling.

DE KONINCK
DE KONINCK

Belgian ale. Stunning peppery hop aroma balanced by rich malt, spicy hop, tart fruit and malt in the mouth, long fruity finish becoming dry and hoppy. The name means "the king" and who would disagree? The copper-coloured ale has the fruitiness of an English ale and the smooth drinkability of a German Alt.

ORIGINAL GRAVITY 1048   11.9° Plato

	25 litres	23 litres	5 UK gals	5 US gals
Lager malt (Pilsen)	4,000 gm	3,700 gm	8.0 lb	6.65 lb
Vienna malt	1,300 gm	1,200 gm	2.55 lb	2.1 lb
Chocolate malt	55 gm	50 gm	1.7 oz	1.4 oz

START OF BOIL

Saaz hops	55 gm	50 gm	1.8 oz	1.5 oz

LAST 15 MINUTES OF BOIL

Irish moss	10 gm	10 gm	.35 oz	.30 oz

BREWING METHOD
Temperature-stepped infusion or single-decoction mash. Top-working yeast

MASH SCHEDULE	50°C - 30 minutes (122°F)	
	67°C - 60 minutes (153°F)	
BOIL TIME	90 minutes	
RACKING GRAVITY	1011	2.7° Plato
ALCOHOL CONTENT	5.0% by volume	3.9% by weight
BITTERNESS	24 EBU	
COLOUR	22 EBC	

DONNINGTON
SBA

English cask-conditioned ale. Warm tannic aroma with fruit notes developing. Rich rounded balance of malt and hop. Dry finish with hints of fruit.

ORIGINAL GRAVITY	1044	10.9° Plato	

	25 litres	23 litres	5 UK gals	5 US gals
Maris Otter pale malt	4,450 gm	4,100 gm	8.85 lb	7.35 lb
Crystal malt	240 gm	220 gm	7.7 oz	6.4 oz
White sucrose	145 gm	135 gm	4.6 oz	3.9 oz

START OF BOIL

Fuggle hops	85 gm	80 gm	2.8 oz	2.3 oz

LAST 15 MINUTES OF BOIL

Fuggle hops	20 gm	20 gm	.7 oz	.6 oz
Irish moss	10 gm	10 gm	.35 oz	.30 oz

BREWING METHOD
Single-infusion mash; top-fermenting yeast

MASH SCHEDULE	65°C - 90 minutes (149°F)	
BOIL TIME	90 minutes	
RACKING GRAVITY	1009	2.2° Plato
ALCOHOL CONTENT	4.7% by volume	3.7% by weight
BITTERNESS	30 EBU	
COLOUR	18 EBC	

MALT EXTRACT VERSION:
Replace the pale malt with the appropriate quantity of pale coloured malt extract syrup and brew using the instructions given in chapter 8.
25l = 3,400 gm: 23l = 3,100 gm: 5UK = 6.8 lb: 5US = 5.7 lb

DUVEL
DUVEL

Belgian ale. Enticing fruit and hop aroma. Ripe pear-like fruit in the mouth, complex finish with fruit giving way to hop bitterness. Duvel, pronounced doovl, comes from the Moorgat brewery, Belgium.

ORIGINAL GRAVITY	1070	16.9° Plato

	25 litres	23 litres	5 UK gals	5 US gals
Pale malt	6,380 gm	5,870 gm	12.75 lb	10.65 lb
White sucrose	870 gm	800 gm	1.7 lb	1.45 lb

START OF BOIL

Styrian Goldings hops	35 gm	30 gm	1.1 oz	1.0 oz

HALF WAY THROUGH BOIL (45 MINUTES)

Saaz hops	35 gm	30 gm	1.1 oz	1.0 oz

LAST 15 MINUTES OF BOIL

Saaz hops	15 gm	15 gm	.5 oz	.45 oz
Irish moss	10 gm	10 gm	.35 oz	.30 oz

BREWING METHOD
Single-infusion mash; top-fermenting yeast

MASH SCHEDULE	67°C - 90 minutes (152°F)	
BOIL TIME	90 minutes	
RACKING GRAVITY	1010	2.4° Plato
ALCOHOL CONTENT	8.0% by volume	6.3% by weight
BITTERNESS	30 EBU	
COLOUR	10 EBC	

Add the sugar about half way through the boil, the exact timing is unimportant. This pale but deceptively strong beer is available in its commercial form unpasteurised, so it should be straightforward enough to culture the yeast from the bottle. Alternatively, use a good top working yeast. Ferment at 16-22°C (60-72°F).

MALT EXTRACT VERSION:
Replace the pale malt with the appropriate quantity of pale coloured malt extract syrup and brew using the instructions given in chapter 8.
25l = 3,400 gm: 23l = 3,100 gm: 5UK = 6.8 lb: 5US = 5.7 lb

FULLER'S
ESB

English cask-conditioned bitter An explosion of malt hops and Cooper's marmalade. Enormous attack of malt and fruit with hop underlay; profound finish with strong Goldings character and hints of orange, lemon, gooseberry and some tannin.

ORIGINAL GRAVITY   1054   13.3° Plato

	25 litres	23 litres	5 UK gals	5 US gals
Pale malt	4,250 gm	3,910 gm	8.5 lb	7.05 lb
Flaked maize	1,200 gm	1,110 gm	2.4 lb	2.0 lb
Crystal malt	520 gm	475 gm	1.0 lb	13.8 oz

START OF BOIL

	25 litres	23 litres	5 UK gals	5 US gals
Target hops (seeded)	16 gm	15 gm	.5 oz	.4 oz
Challenger hops	17 gm	16 gm	.6 oz	.5 oz
Northdown hops (seeded)	17 gm	15 gm	.6 oz	.5 oz

LAST 15 MINUTES OF BOIL

	25 litres	23 litres	5 UK gals	5 US gals
Golding hops	20 gm	20 gm	.7 oz	.6 oz
Irish moss	10 gm	10 gm	.35 oz	.30 oz

BREWING METHOD
Single-infusion mash; top-fermenting yeast

MASH SCHEDULE	67°C - 90 minutes (153°F)
BOIL TIME	90 minutes
RACKING GRAVITY	1012 3.0° Plato
ALCOHOL CONTENT	5.6% by volume 4.4% by weight
BITTERNESS	35 EBU
COLOUR	30 EBC

Fuller, apparently, throw a bucketful of yeast into the copper during the boil, probably as a yeast nutrient for the subsequent fermentation.

HELLER
KÖLSCH

German Kölsch beer brewed in Cologne. Delicate floral hop and sweet malt aroma, gentle hop in the mouth, some fruit in the finish that becomes dry. Golden coloured, top-fermenting beer.

ORIGINAL GRAVITY	1048	11.9° Plato

	25 litres	23 litres	5 UK gals	5 US gals
Lager malt (Pilsen)	4,600 gm	4,200 gm	9.1 lb	7.6 lb
Wheat malt	800 gm	750 gm	1.6 lb	1.3 lb
START OF BOIL				
Hallertau hops	50 gm	45 gm	1.6 oz	1.3 oz
LAST 15 MINUTES OF BOIL				
Irish moss	10 gm	10 gm	.35 oz	.30 oz

BREWING METHOD
Temperature-stepped infusion mash Top-fermenting yeast

MASH SCHEDULE	50°C - 30 minutes (122°F)	
	66°C - 60 minutes (150°F)	
BOIL TIME	90 minutes	
RACKING GRAVITY	1011	2.7° Plato
ALCOHOL CONTENT	5.0% by volume	3.9% by weight
BITTERNESS	28 EBU	
COLOUR	5 EBC	

Kölsch is regarded as a mixed style because it uses a mixture of techniques. Although Kölsch is top-fermented, it is sometimes infusion mashed and sometimes single decoction mashed, but characteristically features a lagering period of three to six weeks at 4°C (39°F). Fermentation temperature should be 16-22°C (60-72°F). For those that prefer a single infusion mash, replace the lager malt with pale malt and mash at 66°C (150°F) for 90 minutes. Any decent "real ale" yeast will give good results.

HIGHGATE BREWERY
HIGHGATE MILD

English cask-conditioned mild ale. Tempting aroma of malt and gentle hop resin, chocolate and coffee notes developing. Chewy malt and light fruit with dry nutty finish. A beautifully made, luscious dark mild.

ORIGINAL GRAVITY	1035	8.8° Plato	

	25 litres	23 litres	5 UK gals	5 US gals
Pale malt	2,600 gm	2,400 gm	5.1 lb	4.25 lb
Crystal malt	380 gm	350 gm	12.1 oz	10.1 oz
Torrefied barley	220 gm	200 gm	7.1 oz	5.9 oz
Black malt	100 gm	90 gm	3.2 oz	2.6 oz
White sucrose	440 gm	400 gm	14.1 oz	11.8 oz

START OF BOIL

	25 litres	23 litres	5 UK gals	5 US gals
Golding hops	55 gm	50 gm	1.7 oz	1.5 oz

LAST 15 MINUTES OF BOIL

	25 litres	23 litres	5 UK gals	5 US gals
Irish moss	10 gm	10 gm	.35 oz	.30 oz

BREWING METHOD
Single-temperature infusion mash; top-working yeast

MASH SCHEDULE	65°C - 90 minutes (149°F)	
BOIL TIME	90 minutes	
RACKING GRAVITY	1006	1.5° Plato
ALCOHOL CONTENT	3.9% by volume	3.1% by weight
BITTERNESS	22 EBU	
COLOUR	63 EBC	

IND COOPE
DOUBLE DIAMOND

English bottled pale ale. Rich fruit and hop aroma. Malt in the mouth, big finish with great hop character, refreshing for a beer of its gravity.

ORIGINAL GRAVITY	1053	13.0° Plato		

	25 litres	23 litres	5 UK gals	5 US gals
Pale malt	5,230 gm	4,810 gm	10.45 lb	8.7 lb
Crystal malt	370 gm	340 gm	11.9 oz	9.9 oz
Flaked maize	295 gm	270 gm	9.4 oz	7.8 oz

START OF BOIL

	25 litres	23 litres	5 UK gals	5 US gals
Target hops (seeded)	40 gm	35 gm	1.3 oz	1.1 oz

LAST 15 MINUTES OF BOIL

	25 litres	23 litres	5 UK gals	5 US gals
Golding hops	15 gm	15 gm	.55 oz	.45 oz
Irish moss	10 gm	10 gm	.35 oz	.30 oz

BREWING METHOD
Single-infusion mash; top-fermenting yeast

MASH SCHEDULE	67°C - 90 minutes (153°F)	
BOIL TIME	90 minutes	
RACKING GRAVITY	1012	2.9° Plato
ALCOHOL CONTENT	5.5% by volume	4.3% by weight
BITTERNESS	35 EBU	
COLOUR	25 EBC	

When told that Double Diamond was still popular abroad, I treated the statement with bemused disbelief, but then I was unaware that the export stuff was OG 1053. It's a bit different from the flavourless, gassy keggyflade of around OG 1036 that used to be marketed under the same brand name in Britain. I have been reliably informed by someone with a great many years more drinking experience than I have, that before the keg revolution Double Diamond available in Britain was a fairly strong drink of similar or even higher gravity, and that there were Single Diamond and Triple Diamond beers as well. Single, Double, and Triple were once used as notation for different strength beers in Britain as they still are in some European countries. Triple Diamond is, apparently, still available in Italy.

JENLAIN
BIÈRE DE GARDE

French style ale. Malt, fruit and peppery hop aromas. Rich malt in the mouth, bitter-sweet finish with liquorice notes. A classic bière de garde, amber coloured, a superb balance between malt, fruit and hops. From Brasserie Duyck, Jenlain, France.

ORIGINAL GRAVITY	1068	16.5° Plato		

	25 litres	23 litres	5 UK gals	5 US gals
Pale malt	6,600 gm	6,050 gm	13.15 lb	10.95 lb
Amber malt	700 gm	650 gm	1.4 lb	1.2 lb
Crystal malt	300 gm	280 gm	9.8 oz	8.2 oz

START OF BOIL

Saaz hops	60 gm	55 gm	1.9 oz	1.6 oz

LAST 15 MINUTES OF BOIL

Irish moss	10 gm	10 gm	.35 oz	.30 oz

BREWING METHOD
Single-infusion mash; top fermented

MASH SCHEDULE	65°C - 90 minutes (149°F)	
BOIL TIME	90 minutes	
RACKING GRAVITY	1015	3.7° Plato
ALCOHOL CONTENT	7.1% by volume	5.6% by weight
BITTERNESS	25 EBU	
COLOUR	35 EBC	

At one time all bière de garde was single-temperature infusion mashed and top fermented. Today, most are multi-temperature infusion mashed and some are bottom fermented. Some top-fermented examples still remain. Ferment at 16-22°C (60-72°F). Jenlain is matured for one month. The bottled version is corked, with real corks rather than crown caps, and is available unpasteurised.

LIEFMANS
GOUDENBAND

*Belgian brown ale. Rich fruit and peppery hop aroma. Ripe fruit
and chocolate in the mouth, dry slightly sour finish. A world
classic brown ale of great complexity. From Brouwerij Liefmans,
Oudenaarde, Belgium.*

ORIGINAL GRAVITY	1052	12.8° Plato	

	25 litres	23 litres	5 UK gals	5 US gals
Pale malt	4,100 gm	3,800 gm	8.1 lb	6.7 lb
Flaked maize	700 gm	650 gm	1.4 lb	1.15 lb
Torrefied barley	700 gm	650 gm	1.4 lb	1.15 lb
Crystal malt	300 gm	275 gm	9.5 oz	7.9 oz
Chocolate malt	135 gm	125 gm	4.3 oz	3.6 oz

START OF BOIL

Whitbread Golding hops	25 gm	25 gm	.9 oz	.75 oz
Tettnang hops	20 gm	15 gm	.6 oz	.5 oz

LAST 15 MINUTES OF BOIL

Saaz hops	15 gm	15 gm	.55 oz	.45 oz
Irish moss	10 gm	10 gm	.35 oz	.30 oz

BREWING METHOD
Single-infusion mash; top-fermenting yeast

MASH SCHEDULE	66°C - 90 minutes (150°F)	
BOIL TIME	90 minutes	
RACKING GRAVITY	1012	3.0° Plato
ALCOHOL CONTENT	5.3% by volume	4.2% by weight
BITTERNESS	20 EBU	
COLOUR	60 EBC	

This is a blend of two beers, one of which is four months old; the
other twelve months old. Both are matured in stainless-steel tanks.
The older beer probably acquires some sourness during maturation,
but it is said that the Liefman's yeast strain imparts a slightly sour,
typically Belgian character. This beer is supplied pasteurised in
Britain thus it will not be possible to culture this yeast from a sample
bottle. The yeast apparently originated from Rodenbach, from which
it should be possible to culture the yeast. If the authentic yeast is not
available, any decent real ale yeast should give good results. See
article on soured and vatted ales in the appendices.

McEWAN 80/-
(EIGHTY SHILLING)

Scottish ale. Strong malt character with citric fruit note. Mouth-filling maltiness with dry, slightly fruity finish.

ORIGINAL GRAVITY	1042		10.4° Plato	

	25 litres	23 litres	5 UK gals	5 US gal
Pale malt	3,150 gm	2,900 gm	6.25 lb	5.2 lb
Flaked maize	700 gm	650 gm	1.35 lb	1.15 lb
Flaked wheat	250 gm	220 gm	7.40 oz	6.20 oz
Roast barley	50 gm	45 gm	1.6 oz	1.5 oz
White sucrose	350 gm	325 gm	11.3 oz	9.5 oz
START OF BOIL				
Challenger hops	50 gm	45 gm	1.65 oz	1.35 oz
LAST 15 MINUTES OF BOIL				
Goldings hops	10 gm	10 gm	.35 oz	.30 oz
Irish moss	10 gm	10 gm	.35 oz	.30 oz

BREWING METHOD
Single-infusion mash; top-fermenting yeast

MASH SCHEDULE	67°C - 90 minutes (153°F)	
BOIL TIME	90 minutes	
RACKING GRAVITY	1008	2.0° Plato
ALCOHOL CONTENT	4.6% by volume	3.7% by weight
BITTERNESS	30 EBU	
COLOUR	25 EBC	

NUSSDORF
ST THOMAS

Vienna Altbier. Bronze-coloured beer with a rich perfumy hop aroma, a good balance of malt and hops in the mouth, some tart fruit and delicate hop in the finish that becomes dry.

ORIGINAL GRAVITY 1050 12.3° Plato

	25 litres	23 litres	5 UK gals	5 US gals
Munich malt (light)	2,650 gm	2,450 gm	5.25 lb	4.35 lb
Vienna malt	2,100 gm	2,000 gm	4.2 lb	3.5 lb
Crystal malt	250 gm	230 gm	8.2 oz	6.9 oz
White sucrose	400 gm	350 gm	12.1 oz	10.1 oz

START OF BOIL

	25 litres	23 litres	5 UK gals	5 US gals
Saaz hops	30 gm	25 gm	.9 oz	.8 oz
Hallertau hops	30 gm	30 gm	1.0 oz	.8 oz

LAST 15 MINUTES OF BOIL

	25 litres	23 litres	5 UK gals	5 US gals
Saaz hops	15 gm	15 gm	.5 oz	.45 oz
Irish moss	10 gm	10 gm	.35 oz	.30 oz

BREWING METHOD
Temperature-stepped infusion mash; top fermented

MASH SCHEDULE	50°C - 30 minutes (122°F)	
	66°C - 60 minutes (150°F)	
BOIL TIME	90 minutes	
RACKING GRAVITY	1009	2.2° Plato
ALCOHOL CONTENT	5.5% by volume	4.3% by weight
BITTERNESS	30 EBU	
COLOUR	30 EBC	

RIDLEY
DARK MILD

English cask-conditioned mild ale. Mellow hop aroma. Mellow nut in the mouth, dry finish. Pleasant dark ruby mild.

ORIGINAL GRAVITY	1034	8.5° Plato

	25 litres	23 litres	5 UK gals	5 US gals
Pale malt	3,050 gm	2,800 gm	6.05 lb	5.05 lb
Chocolate malt	175 gm	160 gm	5.5 oz	4.6 oz
White sucrose	360 gm	330 gm	11.5 oz	9.6 oz

START OF BOIL

Golding hops	30 gm	25 gm	1.0 oz	.8 oz
Fuggle hops	35 gm	30 gm	1.1 oz	.9 oz

LAST 15 MINUTES OF BOIL

Irish moss	10 gm	10 gm	.35 oz	.30 oz

BREWING METHOD
Single-temperature infusion mash; top-working yeast

MASH SCHEDULE	65°C - 90 minutes (149°F)	
BOIL TIME	90 minutes	
RACKING GRAVITY	1006	1.5° Plato
ALCOHOL CONTENT	3.7% by volume	2.9% by weight
BITTERNESS	24 EBU	
COLOUR	60 EBC	

MALT EXTRACT VERSION:
Replace the pale malt with the appropriate quantity of pale coloured malt extract syrup and brew using the instructions given in chapter 8.
25l = 2,350 gm: 23l = 2,150 gm: 5UK = 4.7 lb: 5US = 3.9 lb

SAMUEL SMITHS
MUSEUM ALE

*English cask-conditioned pale ale. Rich malt and hop aromas.
Complex balance of malt, light hop and fruit with a grainy
finish.*

ORIGINAL GRAVITY	1050		12.3° Plato	

	25 litres	**23 litres**	**5 UK gals**	**5 US gals**
Pale malt	5,000 gm	4,600 gm	10.0 lb	8.35 lb
Crystal malt	600 gm	550 gm	1.15 lb	15.95 oz

START OF BOIL

Golding hops	25 gm	25 gm	.85 oz	.7 oz
Fuggle hops	45 gm	40 gm	1.45 oz	1.2 oz

LAST 15 MINUTES OF BOIL

Golding hops	10 gm	10 gm	.35 oz	.30 oz
Irish moss	10 gm	10 gm	.35 oz	.30 oz

BREWING METHOD
Single-infusion mash; top-fermenting yeast

MASH SCHEDULE	67°C - 90 minutes (153°F)	
BOIL TIME	90 minutes	
RACKING GRAVITY	1011	2.8° Plato
ALCOHOL CONTENT	5.2% by volume	4.1% by weight
BITTERNESS	30 EBU	
COLOUR	25 EBC	

MALT EXTRACT VERSION:
Replace the pale malt with the appropriate quantity of pale coloured
malt extract syrup and brew using the instructions given in chapter 8.
25l = 3,800 gm: 23l = 3,500 gm: 5UK = 7.7 lb: 5US = 6.4 lb

SAMUEL SMITHS
NUT BROWN ALE

English bottled brown ale. Fine example of a North-east brown ale, russet coloured, with a fruity, estery nose, sweet malt and dark fruit in the mouth, and a finish that starts malty and becomes dry with gentle hops and light fruit.

ORIGINAL GRAVITY   1048   11.9° Plato

	25 litres	23 litres	5 UK gals	5 US gals
Pale malt	4,250 gm	3,900 gm	8.45 lb	7.05 lb
Amber malt	540 gm	500 gm	1.05 lb	14.5 oz
Crystal malt	550 gm	520 gm	1.1 lb	15.0 oz
Chocolate malt	75 gm	70 gm	2.4 oz	2.0 oz

START OF BOIL

Fuggle hops	100 gm	90 gm	3.2 oz	2.6 oz

LAST 15 MINUTES OF BOIL

Golding hops	20 gm	20 gm	.70 oz	.60 oz
Irish moss	10 gm	10 gm	.35 oz	.30 oz

BREWING METHOD
Single-infusion mash; top-fermenting yeast

MASH SCHEDULE	68°C - 90 minutes (154°F)	
BOIL TIME	90 minutes	
RACKING GRAVITY	1011	2.8° Plato
ALCOHOL CONTENT	4.9% by volume	3.9% by weight
BITTERNESS	34 EBU	
COLOUR	65 EBC	

SCOTTISH & NEWCASTLE
NEWCASTLE BROWN ALE

English bottled brown ale. Malt and toffee aroma. Full bodied, malty and slightly sweet in the mouth, pronounced toffee finish.

ORIGINAL GRAVITY	1044		10.9° Plato	

	25 litres	23 litres	5 UK gals	5 US gals
Pale malt	3,450 gm	3,200 gm	6.9 lb	5.75 lb
Crystal malt	700 gm	650 gm	1.35 lb	1.15 lb
White sucrose	470 gm	430 gm	15.0 oz	12.5 oz
Chocolate malt	40 gm	35 gm	1.3 oz	1.1 oz

START OF BOIL

Target hops (seeded)	15 gm	15 gm	.50 oz	.40 oz
Northern brewer hops	20 gm	20 gm	.70 oz	.60 oz

LAST 15 MINUTES OF BOIL

Irish moss	10 gm	10 gm	.35 oz	.30 oz

BREWING METHOD
Single-infusion mash; top-fermenting yeast

MASH SCHEDULE	67°C - 90 minutes (153°F)	
BOIL TIME	90 minutes	
RACKING GRAVITY	1007	1.7° Plato
ALCOHOL CONTENT	5.0% by volume	3.9% by weight
BITTERNESS	24 EBU	
COLOUR	50 EBC	

Newcastle Brown is a blend of two beers, a strong "vatted" ale, and a weaker beer. The strong beer is matured in maturation tanks for a period of time and this is blended with a weaker and probably younger beer of OG 1030; the final blend having an effective OG of about 1045. Unique flavour characteristics that are only developed during the maturation of strong beers are then imparted to the blended beer, producing a full flavoured beer for its gravity. This technique was used extensively by brewers of old, particularly for producing "running" summer beers, and was known as "bringing forward" in brewerspeak. To imitate the technique brew a 1075 version (multiply all the ingredients in the above recipe by 1.7) and mature it for several weeks. Make a 1030 version (multiply all the ingredients in the above recipe by .68), mature for a week and then blend one third strong to two thirds weak and mature for another week.

SMITHWICK
KILKENNY IRISH BEER

Irish ale. Malt aroma with pear-drop esters. Light malty palate, dry finish with some fruit and hop notes.

ORIGINAL GRAVITY	1048	11.9° Plato

	25 litres	23 litres	5 UK gals	5 US gals
Pale malt	4,870 gm	4,480 gm	9.75 lb	8.1 lb
Crystal malt	495 gm	455 gm	15.78 oz	13.16 oz

START OF BOIL

Challenger hops	30 gm	25 gm	.9 oz	.75 oz
Northdown hops (seeded)	25 gm	25 gm	.85 oz	.70 oz

LAST 15 MINUTES OF BOIL

Fuggle hops	10 gm	10 gm	.35 oz	.35 oz
Irish moss	10 gm	10 gm	.35 oz	.30 oz

LAST 5 MINUTES OF BOIL

Golding hops	10 gm	10 gm	.35 oz	.35 oz

BREWING METHOD
Single-infusion mash; top-fermenting yeast

MASH SCHEDULE	65°C - 90 minutes (149°F)	
BOIL TIME	90 minutes	
RACKING GRAVITY	1011	2.8° Plato
ALCOHOL CONTENT	4.9% by volume	3.9% by weight
BITTERNESS	33 EBU	
COLOUR	30 EBC	

MALT EXTRACT VERSION:
Replace the pale malt with the appropriate quantity of pale coloured malt extract syrup and brew using the instructions given in chapter 8.
25l = 3,750 gm: 23l = 3,450 gm: 5UK = 7.5 lb: 5US = 6.2 lb

ST ARNOULD
RESERVE DU BRASSEUR

Bière de garde. Rich, dark fruit and peppery hops aroma, raisin and sultana fruit in the mouth, big finish packed with dark fruit and spicy hop.

ORIGINAL GRAVITY	1062	15.1° Plato		

	25 litres	**23 litres**	**5 UK gals**	**5 US gals**
Munich malt (light)	3,900 gm	3,600 gm	7.75 lb	6.45 lb
Vienna malt	2,850 gm	2,650 gm	5.7 lb	4.75 lb
Crystal malt	185 gm	170 gm	6.0 oz	5.0 oz

START OF BOIL

Northern brewer hops	20 gm	20 gm	.7 oz	.6 oz
Fuggle hops	35 gm	30 gm	1.2 oz	1.0 oz

LAST 15 MINUTES OF BOIL

Irish moss	10 gm	10 gm	.35 oz	.30 oz

BREWING METHOD
Temperature-stepped infusion mash; top fermented

MASH SCHEDULE	50°C - 30 minutes (122°F)	
	65°C - 60 minutes (149°F)	
BOIL TIME	90 minutes	
RACKING GRAVITY	1014	3.4° Plato
ALCOHOL CONTENT	6.4% by volume	5.0% by weight
BITTERNESS	25 EBU	
COLOUR	35 EBC	

ST SYLVESTRE
3 MONTS

Bière de garde. This French beer exhibits malt, fruit and light hop aromas. Rich malt in the mouth, long dry finish with fruit, hop, coffee and liquorice notes. Rounded, well-balanced between malt and hop. This beer is labelled as bière de Flandre, but in my view it is a bière de garde because it uses a top working yeast. After all, we cannot have the French inventing new beer styles just when the mood suits them. From Brasserie St Sylvester, Cappel, France.

ORIGINAL GRAVITY	1079	19° Plato

	25 litres	23 litres	5 UK gals	5 US gals
Lager malt (Pilsen)	8,200 gm	7,550 gm	16.4 lb	13.7 lb
White sucrose	340 gm	315 gm	11.0 oz	9.1 oz
START OF BOIL				
Brewers Gold hops	20 gm	20 gm	.7 oz	.6 oz
Tettnang hops	35 gm	30 gm	1.0 oz	.9 oz
LAST 15 MINUTES OF BOIL				
Irish moss	10 gm	10 gm	.35 oz	.30 oz

BREWING METHOD
Temperature-stepped infusion mash; top fermented

MASH SCHEDULE	50°C - 30 minutes (122°F)
	66°C - 60 minutes (150°F)
BOIL TIME	90 minutes
RACKING GRAVITY	1016	3.7° Plato
ALCOHOL CONTENT	8.5% by volume	6.7% by weight
BITTERNESS	27 EBU
COLOUR	6 EBC

The brewery did not specify the type of mash employed, but as it specified Pilsner malt, a protein rest period is appropriate. However, as this beer is not supposed to be served highly chilled, a simple decoction mash at 66°C for 90 minutes can probably be used with little risk of a haze being formed; the sugar will also help to dilute any haze potential. Ferment between 16-22°C (60-72°F).

TOLLY COBBOLD
MILD

English cask-conditioned mild ale. Good malt and chocolate aroma. Dark malt in the mouth, dry finish with chocolate and hop notes. A distinctive dark ale.

ORIGINAL GRAVITY	1032	8.0° Plato	

	25 litres	23 litres	5 UK gals	5 US gals
Pale malt	3,060 gm	2,810 gm	6.1 lb	5.1 lb
Crystal malt	360 gm	330 gm	11.5 oz	9.6 oz
Chocolate malt	180 gm	165 gm	5.8 oz	4.8 oz

START OF BOIL

Challenger hops	18 gm	16 gm	.6 oz	.5 oz
Northdown (seeded) hops	11 gm	10 gm	.4 oz	.3 oz

LAST 15 MINUTES OF BOIL

Irish moss	10 gm	10 gm	.35 oz	.30 oz

BREWING METHOD
Single-temperature infusion mash; top-working yeast

MASH SCHEDULE	65°C - 90 minutes (149°F)	
BOIL TIME	90 minutes	
RACKING GRAVITY	1009	2.1° Plato
ALCOHOL CONTENT	3.1% by volume	2.5% by weight
BITTERNESS	18 EBU	
COLOUR	79 EBC	

MALT EXTRACT VERSION:
Replace the pale malt with the appropriate quantity of pale coloured malt extract syrup and brew using the instructions given in chapter 8. 25l = 2,350 gm: 23l = 2,150 gm: 5UK = 4.7 lb: 5US = 3.9 lb

WESTMALLE
DUBBEL

Belgian Trappist beer. Massive peppery hop aroma and fruit notes. Great hop and malt attack in the mouth. Lingering dry finish with fruit notes. It is wonderfully ripe and complex beer, the benchmark for other "double" beers in Belgium. From the Abbdij der Trappisten, Westmalle, Belgium.

ORIGINAL GRAVITY	1064		15.6° Plato	

	25 litres	23 litres	5 UK gals	5 US gals
Lager malt (Pilsen)	6,500 gm	6,000 gm	13.0 lb	10.85 lb
Chocolate malt	155 gm	145 gm	5.0 oz	4.2 oz
White sucrose	300 gm	250 gm	8.9 oz	7.4 oz

START OF BOIL

	25 litres	23 litres	5 UK gals	5 US gals
Styrian Goldings hops	10 gm	10 gm	.35 oz	.30 oz
Saaz hops	20 gm	20 gm	.70 oz	.50 oz
Tettnang hops	15 gm	15 gm	.55 oz	.45 oz

LAST 15 MINUTES OF BOIL

	25 litres	23 litres	5 UK gals	5 US gals
Irish moss	10 gm	10 gm	.35 oz	.30 oz

BREWING METHOD
Temperature-stepped infusion mash; top fermented

MASH SCHEDULE	50°C - 30 minutes (122°F)	
	66°C - 60 minutes (150°F)	
BOIL TIME	90 minutes	
RACKING GRAVITY	1013	3.2° Plato
ALCOHOL CONTENT	6.8% by volume	5.3% by weight
BITTERNESS	20 EBU	
COLOUR	55 EBC	

MALT EXTRACT VERSION:
Replace the pale malt with the appropriate quantity of pale coloured malt extract syrup and brew using the instructions given in chapter 8.
25l = 5,000 gm: 23l = 4,600 gm: 5UK = 10.0 lb: 5US = 8.3 lb

ZUM UERIGE
ALT

Dusseldorf Altbier. The finest of the Alt beers brewed in the "cranky fellow" bar. It is copper-coloured with a rich fruit and hops aroma, dark fruit in the mouth, and an assertively hoppy and dry finish.

ORIGINAL GRAVITY	1048	11.9° Plato

	25 litres	23 litres	5 UK gals	5 US gals
Munich malt (light)	3,500 gm	3,200 gm	6.95 lb	5.8 lb
Vienna malt	1,400 gm	1,300 gm	2.75 lb	2.3 lb
Crystal malt	510 gm	470 gm	1.0 lb	13.6 oz

START OF BOIL				
Saaz hops	115 gm	105 gm	3.7 oz	3.1 oz

LAST 15 MINUTES OF BOIL				
Irish moss	10 gm	10 gm	.35 oz	.30 oz

BREWING METHOD
Temperature-stepped infusion mash. Top-fermenting yeast

MASH SCHEDULE	50°C - 30 minutes (122°F)	
	65°C - 60 minutes (149°F)	
BOIL TIME	90 minutes	
RACKING GRAVITY	1011	2.7° Plato
ALCOHOL CONTENT	5.0% by volume	3.9% by weight
BITTERNESS	48 EBU	
COLOUR	45 EBC	

Stout and Porter

Porter, with its stronger cousin stout, is the born-again beer. A style that spawned the modern commercial brewing industry in Britain was exported widely to the Baltic states – where Imperial Russian Stout became a cult drink at the court of the Czar – and to the colonies. The impact of porter and stout can be measured by its continuing popularity in Africa, where Guinness is a mass brand, the Caribbean and Sri Lanka. A Scot named David Carnegie took the art of porter brewing to Sweden and the style survives today in Scandinavia. Porter-type beers pop up in the most unexpected places, suggesting that seafarers must have taken copious amounts of the ale with them on journeys as far away as Asia. Perhaps even the black beers of Japan may have been influenced by porter, though the dark lagers of Bavaria are a more likely source.

The first porters were blended beers, using pale, brown and 'stale' ales, stale being a term used to describe vatted ales stored for a year or more in unlined wooden tuns. During maturation, the ales were attacked by Brettanomyces wild yeasts, which gave a sour, lactic tang to the blended beer and a slightly musty, old sacks aroma described by brewers as 'horse blanket'. Guinness Foreign Export Stout is still made in this way, with two old wooden vats hidden away in the modern, stainless steel brewery in Dublin.

The origins of porter are hotly disputed. For a lengthy dissertation on the subject, see Roger Protz's 'The Ale Trail'. Suffice it to say here that porter did not begin in a brewhouse in East London in 1722, as the legend implies, but evolved from the blending of brown London beers with the more expensive pale and stale ales produced by country brewers. Entire Butt and porter, considered by most writers and historians to be synonymous, were not even the same beer for most of the 18th and 19th centuries. As a photograph in The Ale Trail shows, such a leading practitioner as Whitbread was offering both Entire and London Porter in London ale houses. Porter, for most of its life, remained a blended beer: just as lambic and gueuze brewers in Belgium will blend beers to suit the demands of individual bars, London porter brewers sent the constituent beers to pubs where they were blended by the publican.

The early porters and entires were almost certainly brown rather than black in colour. Jet-black porters and stouts became possible only with the development of roasting machines in the early 19th century that enabled black and chocolate malts to be made. As units of bitterness were not recorded, it is difficult to say just how bitter and hoppy the first porters, entires and stouts were: certainly large amounts of hops were used, but hop varieties in the 18th and 19th centuries had much lower levels of alpha acids than modern varieties.

Porter and stout production largely disappeared from Britain during World War One when restrictions were placed on the use of barley malt for brewing, especially heavily kilned and roasted malts that used forms of energy – coal, gas and electricity – considered vital to the war effort. No such restrictions were placed on the rebellious Irish. By the time most of Ireland had achieved its nationhood in the 1920s, it dominated the porter market and dry Irish stout became a style unique to that country. Arthur Guinness used a proportion of unmalted roasted barley in his porters to avoid paying too much malt tax to the British government. What began as a tax dodge became the hallmark of the Irish style.

Today porters and stouts are being brewed again with great enthusiasm by brewers in Britain, Europe and the United States. The descendants of Samuel Whitbread in England have recreated an 1850s version of porter as the dark beer sector of the beer market, dominated by Guinness, continues to grow. Craft brewers in the United States have delved deep into history books to replicate the style. We will never know for certain precisely what those original entires, porters and stouts tasted like but we can have enormous pleasure in brewing their modern equivalents.

ARCEN
ARCENER STOUT

Dutch stout. Rich malt and chocolate notes, coffee and chocolate in the mouth, dry and bitter finish. A pleasingly rounded stout dominated by the dark malts.

ORIGINAL GRAVITY   1065   15.8° Plato

	25 litres	23 litres	5 UK gals	5 US gals
Pale malt	5,250 gm	4,800 gm	10.45 lb	8.7 lb
Munich malt (light)	1,600 gm	1,500 gm	3.15 lb	2.65 lb
Chocolate malt	420 gm	385 gm	13.45 oz	11.25 oz

START OF BOIL

	25 litres	23 litres	5 UK gals	5 US gals
Northern brewer hops	25 gm	20 gm	.75 oz	.6 oz
Hallertau hops	25 gm	20 gm	.75 oz	.6 oz

BREWING METHOD
Single infusion mash; top fermenting yeast

MASH SCHEDULE	67°C - 90 minutes	
BOIL TIME	90 minutes	
RACKING GRAVITY	1017	4.0° Plato
ALCOHOL CONTENT	6.5% by volume	5.1% by weight
BITTERNESS	27 EBU	
COLOUR	150 EBC	

COURAGE
RUSSIAN IMPERIAL STOUT

English bottle-conditioned stout / barley wine. Fresh leather and pepper hop on the nose. Bitter black chocolate in the mouth with deep, tart, bitter finish.

ORIGINAL GRAVITY	1098	23.1° Plato	

	25 litres	23 litres	5 UK gals	5 US gals
Pale malt	4,300 gm	4,000 gm	8.55 lb	7.15 lb
Lager malt (Pilsen)	3,000 gm	2,800 gm	6.0 lb	5.0 lb
Amber malt	1,500 gm	1,450 gm	3.1 lb	2.55 lb
Black malt	485 gm	445 gm	15.45 oz	12.9 oz
White sucrose	1,000 gm	950 gm	2.05 lb	1.7 lb

START OF BOIL

	25 litres	23 litres	5 UK gals	5 US gals
Target hops (seeded)	60 gm	55 gm	1.85 oz	1.55 oz

BREWING METHOD
Single-infusion mash; top-fermenting yeast

MASH SCHEDULE	67°C - 90 minutes (153°F)	
BOIL TIME	90 minutes	
RACKING GRAVITY	1018	4.3° Plato
ALCOHOL CONTENT	10.7% by volume	8.3% by weight
BITTERNESS	50 EBU	
COLOUR	235 EBC	

Mature in cask for several weeks and then condition in bottle for a minimum of eighteen months. This beer was first brewed by Barclay & Perkins brewery for the Russian Court. The same brewery was at the centre of a storm in 1850 when an Austrian leader, General Haynau, visited the brewery. Haynau had put down the Hungarian revolt with extreme brutality and his methods included the public flogging of Italian and Hungarian women as reprisal. On his visit to the brewery the draymen and other brewery workers mobbed him and proceeded to "rough him up". He was rescued after having his clothes torn and half his beard pulled out, but Lord Palmerston, the Foreign Secretary at the time, said that the mob should have "tossed him in a horse blanket, rolled him the kennel (the street gutter), and then sent him home in a cab."

ELDRIDGE POPE
GOLDIE BARLEY WINE

English strong ale. Full malt and fruit with peppery hop notes. Warming malt in the mouth, massive fruit and hop finish with a good clean bitterness. Rich sherry-like character.

ORIGINAL GRAVITY	1090	21.4° Plato	

	25 litres	23 litres	5 UK gals	5 US gals
Maris Otter pale malt	6,500 gm	6,000 gm	12.95 lb	10.8 lb
Lager malt (Pilsen)	3,500 gm	3,200 gm	6.95 lb	5.8 lb

START OF BOIL

Golding hops	40 gm	35 gm	1.25 oz	1.0 oz
Fuggle hops	45 gm	40 gm	1.45 oz	1.2 oz
Styrian Goldings hops	25 gm	25 gm	.8 oz	.65 oz

LAST 15 MINUTES OF BOIL

Irish moss	10 gm	10 gm	.35 oz	.30 oz

BREWING METHOD
Single infusion mash; top fermenting yeast

MASH SCHEDULE	68°C - 90 minutes (154°F)	
BOIL TIME	90 minutes	
RACKING GRAVITY	1020	4.8° Plato
ALCOHOL CONTENT	9.4% by volume	7.3% by weight
BITTERNESS	45 EBU	
COLOUR	13 EBC	

GEORGE GALE
NOURISHING STOUT

English stout. Malt and coffee aromas. Light toasted malt in the mouth, bitter-sweet finish becoming dry.

ORIGINAL GRAVITY	1048	11.9° Plato

	25 litres	23 litres	5 UK gals	5 US gals
Pale malt	3,800 gm	3,500 gm	7.6 lb	6.35 lb
Torrefied wheat	800 gm	750 gm	1.55 lb	1.3 lb
Black malt	330 gm	300 gm	10.55 oz	8.8 oz
White sucrose	315 gm	290 gm	10.05 oz	8.35 oz
START OF BOIL				
Challenger hops	15 gm	10 gm	.4 oz	.3 oz
Golding hops	15 gm	15 gm	.55 oz	.45 oz
Fuggle hops	20 gm	20 gm	.7 oz	.55 oz

BREWING METHOD
Single infusion mash; top fermenting yeast

MASH SCHEDULE	66°C - 90 minutes (151°F)	
BOIL TIME	90 minutes	
RACKING GRAVITY	1011	2.7° Plato
ALCOHOL CONTENT	5.0% by volume	3.9% by weight
BITTERNESS	22 EBU	
COLOUR	144 EBC	

Add the sucrose to the copper during the last half-hour of the boil. So called "food" stouts were very popular at one time due to their supposed nutritional benefit. Medical journals of the early twentieth century expounded greatly on the health-giving and nutritional properties of beer, particularly stouts. Medical doctors were under the misguided impression that stouts are rich in iron and had the habit of prescribing them to poorly old ladies.

GUINNESS
EXPORT STOUT

Irish stout. Pronounced roast barley notes and enormous hop character. Complex bitter-sweet balance of roast barley, fruit and hop. Immense finish with coffee and chocolate notes and hop bitterness.

| **ORIGINAL GRAVITY** | 1048 | 11.9° Plato | |

	25 litres	**23 litres**	**5 UK gals**	**5 US gals**
Pale malt	3,900 gm	3,600 gm	7.8 lb	6.5 lb
Flaked barley	1,500 gm	1,050 gm	2.2 lb	1.85 lb
Roast barley	500 gm	460 gm	15.95 oz	13.3 oz

START OF BOIL

	25 litres	**23 litres**	**5 UK gals**	**5 US gals**
Target hops (seeded)	30 gm	30 gm	1.0 oz	.85 oz
Golding hops	45 gm	40 gm	1.4 oz	1.15 oz

BREWING METHOD
Single-infusion mash; top fermenting yeast

MASH SCHEDULE	67°C - 90 minutes (153°F)	
BOIL TIME	90 minutes	
RACKING GRAVITY	1014	3.5° Plato
ALCOHOL CONTENT	4.6% by volume	3.6% by weight
BITTERNESS	45 EBU	
COLOUR	200 EBC	

GUINNESS
FOREIGN EXTRA STOUT

Strong Irish stout. A world classic, its roots in the early porters and stouts of London and Dublin. The beer is a blend of regular stout and a second beer that is matured in unlined oak vessels for around two months. It has the "horse-blanket" aroma that is the result of attack from wild Brettanomyces yeasts in the vats, a rich and spicy fruitiness and great depth of hop bitterness. Dark fruit and hops dominate the mouth, while the finish is full of complex sour fruit, malt and hops. The yeast strain used in the Dublin brewery is a modern culture derived from Arthur Guinness's original multi-strain one. It works rapidly, fermentation lasting only two to three days and is neither top nor bottom fermenting – quite a challenge for home brewers.

ORIGINAL GRAVITY	1073	17.6° Plato

	25 litres	23 litres	5 UK gals	5 US gals
Pale malt	6,200 gm	5,700 gm	12.4 lb	10.35 lb
Flaked barley	1,700 gm	1,550 gm	3.35 lb	2.8 lb
Roast barley	500 gm	450 gm	15.7 oz	13.1 oz

START OF BOIL

Target hops (seeded)	45 gm	40 gm	1.45 oz	1.2 oz
Golding hops	65 gm	60 gm	2.05 oz	1.7 oz

BREWING METHOD
Single-infusion mash; top fermenting yeast

MASH SCHEDULE	67°C - 90 minutes (153°F)	
BOIL TIME	90 minutes	
RACKING GRAVITY	1020	4.7° Plato
ALCOHOL CONTENT	7.2% by volume	5.6% by weight
BITTERNESS	65 EBU	
COLOUR	200 EBC	

MACKESON
EXPORT STOUT

English milk stout. "Milk stout" has an undeserved reputation of being sweet. This ruby-black beer is far from sweet, though the use of lactose leaves some unfermented sugars in the beer for body. It has a rich and darkly fruity aroma, a creamy flavour with a hint of "milk drops" sweets, and a big finish packed with dark fruit, liquorice and gentle hops.

ORIGINAL GRAVITY	1059		14.4° Plato	

	25 litres	23 litres	5 UK gals	5 US gals
Pale malt	4,750 gm	4,400 gm	9.5 lb	7.95 lb
Chocolate malt	700 gm	650 gm	1.35 lb	1.15 lb
Black malt	170 gm	150 gm	5.35 oz	4.45 oz
Lactose	650 gm	600 gm	1.25 lb	1.05 lb

START OF BOIL

Target hops (seeded)	40 gm	35 gm	1.25 oz	1.05 oz

BREWING METHOD
Single-infusion mash; top-fermenting yeast

MASH SCHEDULE	67°C - 90 minutes (153°F)	
BOIL TIME	90 minutes	
RACKING GRAVITY	1025	6.0° Plato
ALCOHOL CONTENT	4.6% by volume	3.6% by weight
BITTERNESS	34 EBU	
COLOUR	300 EBC	

The lactose should be added to the boiler during the last half-hour of the boil. The exceptionally high racking gravity is to be expected and is due to the non-fermentable lactose.

MALT EXTRACT VERSION:
Replace the pale malt with the appropriate quantity of pale coloured malt extract syrup and brew using the instructions given in chapter 8. 25l = 3,650 gm: 23l = 3,350 gm: 5UK = 7.3 lb: 5US = 6.1 lb

MACKESON
STOUT

English sweet stout (milk stout). A restrained version of the export stout, with a fruity aroma, sweet dark malt and fruit in the mouth, a hint of milk drops and liquorice in the finish.

ORIGINAL GRAVITY   1042   10.4° Plato

	25 litres	23 litres	5 UK gals	5 US gals
Pale malt	3,070 gm	2,830 gm	6.15 lb	5.1 lb
Chocolate malt	510 gm	470 gm	1.0 lb	13.7 oz
Black malt	135 gm	125 gm	4.25 oz	3.55 oz
Lactose	630 gm	580 gm	1.25 lb	1.05 lb

START OF BOIL

	25 litres	23 litres	5 UK gals	5 US gals
Target hops (seeded)	30 gm	30 gm	.95 oz	.8 oz

BREWING METHOD
Single-infusion mash; top-fermenting yeast

MASH SCHEDULE	67°C - 90 minutes (153°F)	
BOIL TIME	90 minutes	
RACKING GRAVITY	1020	5.0° Plato
ALCOHOL CONTENT	3.0% by volume	2.3% by weight
BITTERNESS	26 EBU	
COLOUR	225 EBC	

The lactose should be added to the boiler during the last half-hour of the boil. The high racking gravity is to be expected and is due to the non-fermentable lactose.

MALT EXTRACT VERSION:
Replace the pale malt with the appropriate quantity of pale coloured malt extract syrup and brew using the instructions given in chapter 8. 25l = 2,350 gm: 23l = 2,200 gm: 5UK = 4.7 lb: 5US = 3.9 lb

MURPHY
STOUT

Irish dry stout. Light aroma of roasted grain and gentle hops, dark and creamy malt in the mouth, gentle malt and hops in the finish with hints of chocolate. Most easy-drinking and undemanding of the Irish stouts.

ORIGINAL GRAVITY   1038   9.5° Plato

	25 litres	23 litres	5 UK gals	5 US gals
Pale malt	2,850 gm	2,650 gm	5.7 lb	4.75 lb
Roast barley	400 gm	350 gm	12.5 oz	10.45 oz
Chocolate malt	80 gm	70 gm	2.5 oz	2.05 oz
White sucrose	600 gm	550 gm	1.15 lb	15.65 oz

START OF BOIL

Target hops (seeded)	40 gm	35 gm	1.3 oz	1.1 oz

BREWING METHOD
Single-infusion mash; top-fermenting yeast

MASH SCHEDULE	66°C - 90 minutes (151°F)	
BOIL TIME	90 minutes	
RACKING GRAVITY	1008	1.9° Plato
ALCOHOL CONTENT	4.1% by volume	3.2% by weight
BITTERNESS	35 EBU	
COLOUR	180 EBC	

MALT EXTRACT VERSION:
Replace the pale malt with the appropriate quantity of pale coloured malt extract syrup and brew using the instructions given in chapter 8.
25l =2,200 gm: 23l = 2,000 gm: 5UK = 4.4 lb: 5US = 3.6 lb

SAMUEL SMITH
IMPERIAL STOUT

English stout. Big and complex aroma of dark fruit, peppery hops and roasted malt, rich fruit and malt in the mouth, long finish dominated by hops, raisin fruit and dark, roasted grain.

ORIGINAL GRAVITY   1072   17.4° Plato

	25 litres	23 litres	5 UK gals	5 US gals
Pale malt	6,170 gm	5,680 gm	12.35 lb	10.3 lb
Crystal malt	620 gm	570 gm	1.2 lb	1.0 lb
Roast barley	300 gm	280 gm	9.65 oz	8.05 oz
White sucrose	620 gm	570 gm	1.2 lb	1.0 lb
START OF BOIL				
Golding hops	60 gm	55 gm	1.95 oz	1.65 oz
Fuggle hops	70 gm	65 gm	2.3 oz	1.95 oz

BREWING METHOD
Single-infusion mash; top fermenting yeast

MASH SCHEDULE	66°C - 90 minutes (151°F)	
BOIL TIME	90 minutes	
RACKING GRAVITY	1015	3.6° Plato
ALCOHOL CONTENT	7.7% by volume	6.0% by weight
BITTERNESS	50 EBU	
COLOUR	155 EBC	

MALT EXTRACT VERSION:
Replace the pale malt with the appropriate quantity of pale coloured malt extract syrup and brew using the instructions given in chapter 8.
25l = 4,750 gm: 23l = 4,350 gm: 5UK = 9.5 lb: 5US = 7.9 lb

SAMUEL SMITH
OATMEAL STOUT

English food stout. Creamy malt and gentle hops aroma, sweet malt and fruit in the mouth, lingering finish with delicate hops, dark fruit and sweet grain with a hint of chocolate.

ORIGINAL GRAVITY	1048	11.9° Plato	

	25 litres	23 litres	5 UK gals	5 US gals
Pale malt	4,760 gm	4,380 gm	9.5 lb	7.9 lb
Chocolate malt	285 gm	260 gm	9.1 oz	7.6 oz
Black malt	135 gm	125 gm	4.3 oz	3.6 oz
Flaked oats	335 gm	310 gm	10.7 oz	8.95 oz

START OF BOIL

	25 litres	23 litres	5 UK gals	5 US gals
Challenger hops	25 gm	25gm	.8 oz	.65 oz
Fuggle hops	45 gm	40 gm	1.4 oz	1.15 oz

BREWING METHOD
Single-infusion mash; top-fermenting yeast

MASH SCHEDULE	66°C - 90 minutes (151°F)	
BOIL TIME	90 minutes	
RACKING GRAVITY	1013	3.2° Plato
ALCOHOL CONTENT	4.7% by volume	3.7% by weight
BITTERNESS	30 EBU	
COLOUR	155 EBC	

SINEBRYCHOFF
PORTER

Finnish porter. Big earthy hops and dark fruit on the aroma, fruit and chocolate in the mouth, big finish packed with bitter hops, dark grain, tart fruit and chocolate.

ORIGINAL GRAVITY	1068	16.5° Plato

	25 litres	23 litres	5 UK gals	5 US gals
Pale malt	6,270 gm	5,770 gm	12.5 lb	10.45 lb
Crystal malt	760 gm	700 gm	1.5 lb	1.25 lb
Chocolate malt	640 gm	590 gm	1.25 lb	1.05 lb

START OF BOIL

Northern brewer hops	85 gm	80 gm	2.75 oz	2.3 oz

BREWING METHOD
Single-infusion mash; top-fermenting yeast

MASH SCHEDULE	65°C - 90 minutes (149°F)	
BOIL TIME	90 minutes	
RACKING GRAVITY	1019	4.7° Plato
ALCOHOL CONTENT	6.5% by volume	5.1% by weight
BITTERNESS	50 EBU	
COLOUR	250 EBC	

MALT EXTRACT VERSION:
Replace the pale malt with the appropriate quantity of pale coloured malt extract syrup and brew using the instructions given in chapter 8.
25l = 4,800 gm: 23l = 4,450 gm: 5UK = 9.6 lb: 5US = 8.0 lb

SMITHWICK
BARLEY WINE

Irish strong ale. Fruity aroma with good balance of hops, pear drop fruit in the mouth, finish starts rich and sweet, becomes fruity, estery and hoppy.

ORIGINAL GRAVITY 1063   15.3° Plato

	25 litres	23 litres	5 UK gals	5 US gals
Pale malt	5,660 gm	5,210 gm	11.3 lb	9.45 lb
Flaked maize	1050 gm	960 gm	2.05 lb	1.7 lb
Roast barley	235 gm	215 gm	7.5 oz	6.25 oz

START OF BOIL

Challenger hops	32 gm	30 gm	1.05 oz	.85 oz
Northdown hops (seeded)	25 gm	23 gm	.8 oz	.65 oz

LAST 15 MINUTES OF BOIL

Irish moss	10 gm	10 gm	.35 oz	.30 oz

BREWING METHOD
Single-infusion mash; top-fermenting yeast

MASH SCHEDULE	66°C - 90 minutes
BOIL TIME	90 minutes
RACKING GRAVITY	1016 3.8° Plato
ALCOHOL CONTENT	6.4% by volume 5.0% by weight
BITTERNESS	35 EBU
COLOUR	100 EBC

At OG 1063 this is not really strong enough to be regarded as a barley wine, but that is what Smithwicks call it. As barley wine is a fairly meaningless term anyway I will let them have the benefit of the doubt.

WHITBREAD
CASTLE EDEN PORTER

English porter. Based on an 1850 Whitbread London recipe, this superb recreation has a rich chocolate and pungent hops aroma, dark malt and tart fruit in the mouth, and a long finish with chocolate, coffee, dark fruit and peppery hops.

ORIGINAL GRAVITY	1052	12.8° Plato

	25 litres	23 litres	5 UK gals	5 US gals
Pale malt	4,970 gm	4,570 gm	9.9 lb	8.25 lb
Chocolate malt	880 gm	810 gm	1.75 lb	1.45 lb

START OF BOIL

Golding hops	100 gm	90gm	3.15 oz	2.65 oz

BREWING METHOD
Single-infusion mash; top fermenting yeast

MASH SCHEDULE	67°C - 90 minutes (153°F)	
BOIL TIME	90 minutes	
RACKING GRAVITY	1016	3.9° Plato
ALCOHOL CONTENT	4.8% by volume	3.8% by weight
BITTERNESS	40 EBU	
COLOUR	290 EBC	

MALT EXTRACT VERSION:
Replace the pale malt with the appropriate quantity of pale coloured malt extract syrup and brew using the instructions given in chapter 8. 25l = 3,800 gm: 23l = 3,500 gm: 5UK = 7.6 lb: 5US = 6.4 lb

Pale and Pilsner-style Lagers

It seems difficult to believe that a beer style developed in the mid-19th century should be cloaked in mystery, but no one is yet certain how the first Pilsner lager came to have an enticing colour that entranced the world. We know that in 1842 the innkeepers of Pilsen in Bohemia, now the Czech Republic, employed a Bavarian brewer named Josef Groll or Grolle to brew the new-style bottom-fermenting beer in a municipal brewery they had built. According to local legend – as keenly believed as the one that places the first porter in an East London brewpub in 1722 – the maltster charged to make malt for Groll made a mistake in his kiln and produced a pale rather than a brown malt. It is frankly unbelievable. In the first place, any self-respecting brewer would have rejected the wrong type of malt. In the second, the technology had existed for some time to make pale malt. The fact that the Munich brewers who had pioneered lagering on a commercial scale were still making dark or 'dunkel' beers was due more to the deep conservatism of consumers in Bavaria than to any inability to make pale beers.

The most plausible reasons for the arrival of pale lagers in Pilsen were the soft local waters, easy access to the superbly aromatic hops from the Zatec region close to Pilsen, and the move from pewter tankards to glass in the local taverns. Far from being an error, it is likely that the innkeepers had instructed Groll to make a pale beer that would look inviting in glass and would offer a clearly different product to the brown lagers of Munich.

The new Pilsen beer was a sensation. Its clarity was appealing and its complex aromas and flavours, hoppy and malty, appealed to all that drank it. As with pale ale in Britain, but on a larger scale, the fame of the beer was spread by canals and the new railway system. Pilsner beer reached all parts of the Austrian Empire, across into Bavaria and up the Elbe to Hamburg. The second wave of emigrants took both the name and the art of brewing pale lagers to the United States. The term 'Pilsner' was a German style for identifying the origins of a product: the beers from Budweis were similarly known as 'Budweisers'. Sadly, neither towns bothered to register the titles, with the result that Pilsner became the most abused beer style in the world, meaning all too often a thin and undistinguished pale 'international' lager, while Budweiser in its American form is proof of the power of marketing and advertising rather than of intrinsic product quality.

In 1898, but far too late, the first Pilsen lager brewery registered 'Pilsner Urquell' – meaning Original Source Pilsner in German: the Czech is Plzensky Pradroj – as its official name. The document referred to the 'absurdity and illogicality of using the word "Pilsner" for beers brewed in towns outside of Pilsen'. In the Czech Republic the term Pilsner is used as an appellation and only the breweries in Pilsen, Urquell and Gambrinus, can use it. In Germany, where 'Pils' is such a widespread style and where Holsten suggests in its advertising that its beer may be the original Pils, drinkers can be forgiven for thinking their country invented the beer. But the punctilious Germans have decreed that Pils brewers must append either their name or the town of origin to their beers, hence Bitburger Pils or Jever Pils, to avoid confusion with the Czech originals.

A true Pilsner will have great depth of flavour and aroma, with a marriage of maltiness, an almost oaky hint of vanilla and a deep bitterness and citric fruit from the hops. In contrast, a Budweiser will have a more gentle hoppiness, a greater vanilla presence and pronounced malt sweetness. Tragically, the original Pilsner is changing its character as a result of fundamental alterations to the Urquell brewery. Wooden fermenters and lagering tanks have been replaced by stainless steel conicals. The yeast works more vigorously, turning more malt sugars into alcohol. The result is a drier and more bitter beer, more in the German style. The changes have been made as a result of the Czechs being persuaded by the Germans that brewing with wood may be outlawed by the European Union, which the Czechs are anxious to join. The rumour is specious but it has allowed German manufacturers to sell expensive modern brewing vessels to Czech brewers. Ironically, it may be that users of this book will be able to recreate a more genuine Pilsner than the brewers of Pilsen themselves.

AYING
AYINGER JAHRHUNDERTBIER

German Pilsner-type single beer. Massive herbal bouquet. Soft rounded malt and hop in the mouth, long finish with bitter hop notes. From Brauerei Aying, Aying, Germany.

ORIGINAL GRAVITY	1053	13.0° Plato	

	25 litres	23 litres	5 UK gals	5 US gals
Lager malt (Pilsen)	5,900 gm	5,400 gm	11.75 lb	9.8 lb

START OF BOIL

	25 litres	23 litres	5 UK gals	5 US gals
Saaz hops	30 gm	30 gm	1.0 oz	.8 oz
Hallertau hops	10 gm	10 gm	.4 oz	.3 oz
Tettnang hops	15 gm	15 gm	.5 oz	.4 oz

LAST 15 MINUTES OF BOIL

	25 litres	23 litres	5 UK gals	5 US gals
Irish moss	10 gm	10 gm	.35 oz	.30 oz

BREWING METHOD
Temperature-stepped infusion or single-decoction mash. Bottom-fermenting lager yeast

MASH SCHEDULE	50°C - 20 minutes (122°F)	
	65°C - 60 minutes (149°F)	
BOIL TIME	90 minutes	
RACKING GRAVITY	1012	2.9° Plato
ALCOHOL CONTENT	5.5% by volume	4.4% by weight
BITTERNESS	25 EBU	
COLOUR	4 EBC	

Lagered for two months.

MALT EXTRACT VERSION:
Replace the Pilsner malt with the appropriate quantity of pale coloured malt extract syrup and brew using the instructions given in chapter 8.
25l = 4,550 gm: 23l = 4,150 gm: 5UK = 9.0 lb: 5US = 7.5 lb

BITBURGER
PILS

German Pilsner-style lager. Light hop aroma. Dry and delicate hop in the mouth. Finish becomes dry and bitter. One of the best-known Pilsner beers in Germany.

ORIGINAL GRAVITY	1046	11.4° Plato

	25 litres	23 litres	5 UK gals	5 US gals
Lager malt (Pilsen)	4,850 gm	4,500 gm	9.7 lb	8.1 lb

START OF BOIL

Northern brewer hops	65 gm	60 gm	2.0 oz	1.6 oz

HALF WAY THROUGH BOIL (45 MINUTES)

Tettnang hops	25 gm	25 gm	.8 oz	.7 oz

LAST 15 MINUTES OF BOIL

Tettnang hops	15 gm	15 gm	.50 oz	.40 oz
Irish moss	10 gm	10 gm	.35 oz	.30 oz

BREWING METHOD
Temperature-stepped infusion or double-decoction mash. Bottom-fermenting lager yeast

MASH SCHEDULE	52°C - 20 minutes (126°F)	
	63°C - 30 minutes (145°F)	
	72°C - 30 minutes (162°F)	
BOIL TIME	90 minutes	
RACKING GRAVITY	1010	2.6° Plato
ALCOHOL CONTENT	4.8% by volume	3.9% by weight
BITTERNESS	38 EBU	
COLOUR	4 EBC	

Bitberger actually use a double-decoction mash, but the simple two temperature mash described in chapters 6 and 10 will serve just as well. The commercial version of this beer is apparently fermented at 5-7°C (41-45°F) and is lagered for three months.

MALT EXTRACT VERSION:
Replace the Pilsner malt with the appropriate quantity of pale coloured malt extract syrup and brew using the instructions given in chapter 8.
25l = 3,700 gm: 23l = 3,400 gm: 5UK = 7.4 lb: 5US = 6.2 lb

121

BRAND
BRAND PILS

Dutch Pilsner-style lager. A light and refreshing Pilsner sold in a white ceramic-style bottle. Marketed as Royal Brand Beer in North America. Light malt and hop aroma. Delicate malt in the mouth, light dry finish with some hop notes. From the Brand Brewery, Wiljre, The Netherlands.

ORIGINAL GRAVITY	1048	11.9° Plato

	25 litres	23 litres	5 UK gals	5 US gals
Pale malt	4,760 gm	4,380 gm	9.5 lb	7.9 lb
Flaked maize	530 gm	485 gm	1.05 lb	14.1 oz

START OF BOIL

	25 litres	23 litres	5 UK gals	5 US gals
Northern brewer hops	25 gm	20 gm	.8 oz	.6 oz
Perle hops	25 gm	20 gm	.8 oz	.6 oz

LAST 15 MINUTES OF BOIL

	25 litres	23 litres	5 UK gals	5 US gals
Hallertau hops	10 gm	10 gm	.35 oz	.30 oz
Irish moss	10 gm	10 gm	.35 oz	.30 oz

BREWING METHOD
Temperature-stepped infusion or single-decoction mash. Bottom-fermenting lager yeast

MASH SCHEDULE	50°C - 30 minutes (122°F)	
	66°C - 60 minutes (151°F)	
BOIL TIME	90 minutes	
RACKING GRAVITY	1011	2.7° Plato
ALCOHOL CONTENT	5.0% by volume	4.0% by weight
BITTERNESS	27 EBU	
COLOUR	7 EBC	

Lagered for six weeks

BRAND
BRAND UP

Dutch lager. Strong hop and citric fruit aroma. Fine balance of malt and hop, lingering hop and lemon finish. From the Brand brewery, Wijlre, The Netherlands.

ORIGINAL GRAVITY 1051   12.6° Plato

	25 litres	23 litres	5 UK gals	5 US gals
Pale malt	5,650 gm	5,200 gm	11.3 lb	9.4 lb

START OF BOIL

Saaz hops	30 gm	30 gm	1.0 oz	.8 oz
Hallertau hops	20 gm	20 gm	.7 oz	.6 oz
Tettnang hops	30 gm	25 gm	.9 oz	.8 oz

LAST 15 MINUTES OF BOIL

Irish moss	10 gm	10 gm	.35 oz	.30 oz

BREWING METHOD
Temperature-stepped infusion or single-decoction mash. Bottom-fermenting lager yeast

MASH SCHEDULE	50°C - 30 minutes (122°F)	
	66°C - 60 minutes (151°F)	
BOIL TIME	90 minutes	
RACKING GRAVITY	1011	2.8° Plato
ALCOHOL CONTENT	5.3% by volume	4.3% by weight
BITTERNESS	37 EBU	
COLOUR	9 EBC	

Lagered for 7-8 weeks.

MALT EXTRACT VERSION:
Replace the pale malt with the appropriate quantity of pale coloured malt extract syrup and brew using the instructions given in chapter 8.
25l = 4,350 gm: 23l = 4,000 gm: 5UK = 8.7 lb: 5US = 7.2 lb

BUDWEISER
BUDVAR

True Budweis lager. Spritzy aroma of hops and gentle fruit. Quenching, beautifully balanced in the mouth, bitter-sweet finish with light vanilla notes.

| ORIGINAL GRAVITY | 1048 | | 11.9° Plato | |

	25 litres	23 litres	5 UK gals	5 US gals
Lager malt (Pilsen)	5,300 gm	4,900 gm	10.65 lb	8.85 lb
START OF BOIL				
Saaz hops	50 gm	45 gm	1.5 oz	1.3 oz
LAST 15 MINUTES OF BOIL				
Irish moss	10 gm	10 gm	.35 oz	.30 oz

BREWING METHOD
Temperature-stepped infusion or double-decoction mash. Bottom-working lager yeast

MASH SCHEDULE	50°C - 20 minutes (122°F)	
	60°C - 40 minutes (140°F)	
	70°C - 40 minutes (158°F)	
BOIL TIME	90 minutes	
RACKING GRAVITY	1011	2.7° Plato
ALCOHOL CONTENT	5.0% by volume	4.0% by weight
BITTERNESS	20 EBU	
COLOUR	4 EBC	

Lagered for three months.

CARLSBERG
ELEPHANT BEER

Danish strong lager. A seductive pale gold colour leads into a powerful but refreshing beer in which a basic fruitiness is offset by a good hop rate. Yeasty, grainy aroma with fruit notes developing. Orange and tangerine fruit in the mouth, dry finish with some hop character.

ORIGINAL GRAVITY	1065		15.8° Plato	

	25 litres	23 litres	5 UK gals	5 US gals
Lager malt (Pilsen)	5,950 gm	5,450 gm	11.85 lb	9.85 lb
White sucrose	800 gm	750 gm	1.6 lb	1.3 lb
START OF BOIL				
Hallertau hops	65 gm	60 gm	2.1 oz	1.8 oz
LAST 15 MINUTES OF BOIL				
Hallertau hops	15 gm	15 gm	.5 oz	.4 oz
Irish moss	10 gm	10 gm	.35 oz	.30 oz

BREWING METHOD
Temperature-stepped infusion or double-decoction mash. Bottom-working lager yeast

MASH SCHEDULE	50°C - 20 minutes (122°F)	
	66°C - 45 minutes (151°F)	
	72°C - 45 minutes (162°F)	
BOIL TIME	90 minutes	
RACKING GRAVITY	1009	2.3° Plato
ALCOHOL CONTENT	7.5% by volume	6.0% by weight
BITTERNESS	38 EBU	
COLOUR	5 EBC	

MALT EXTRACT VERSION:
Replace the pale malt with the appropriate quantity of pale coloured malt extract syrup and brew using the instructions given in chapter 8. 25l = 4,550 gm: 23l = 4,200 gm: 5UK = 9.0 lb: 5US = 7.6 lb

CARLSBERG
HOF

Danish lager beer. Gentle hops aroma balanced by sweet malt; light hops and malt in the mouth, short dry finish with delicate hops.

ORIGINAL GRAVITY 1041   10.2° Plato

	25 litres	23 litres	5 UK gals	5 US gals
Lager malt (Pilsen)	3,500 gm	3,220 gm	7.0 lb	5.8 lb
Carapils	260 gm	240 gm	8.2 oz	6.8 oz
White sucrose	500 gm	470 gm	1.0 lb	13.7 oz

START OF BOIL

Hallertau hops	40 gm	35 gm	1.3 oz	1.1 oz

LAST 15 MINUTES OF BOIL

Irish moss	10 gm	10 gm	.35 oz	.30 oz

BREWING METHOD
Temperature-stepped infusion or double-decoction mash. Bottom-working lager yeast

MASH SCHEDULE	50°C - 20 minutes (122°F)	
	66°C - 45 minutes (151°F)	
	72°C - 45 minutes (162°F)	
BOIL TIME	90 minutes	
RACKING GRAVITY	1006	1.5° Plato
ALCOHOL CONTENT	4.7% by volume	3.8% by weight
BITTERNESS	23 EBU	
COLOUR	5 EBC	

Carlsberg use the double-decoction mash, but the simple two-temperature stepped mash given in chapter 10 is sufficient. It should be possible, even, to get away with a simple infusion mash. Ferment at 10-15°C (50-59°F), lager at 10°C (50°F).

MALT EXTRACT VERSION:
Replace the Pilsner malt with the appropriate quantity of pale coloured malt extract syrup and brew using the instructions given in chapter 8.
25l = 2,700 gm: 23l = 2,500 gm: 5UK = 5.4 lb: 5US = 4.5 lb

DAB
ORIGINAL

Dortmunder export lager. Malty 'puffed wheat' aroma with light citric notes. Clean and refreshing in the mouth, intense bitter finish with lemon fruit. A fine example of a Dortmunder beer, from one of the great brewing cities of Germany, home to seven commercial producers, of which DAB is the biggest.

ORIGINAL GRAVITY	1048	11.9° Plato

	25 litres	23 litres	5 UK gals	5 US gals
Lager malt (Pilsen)	3,850 gm	3,550 gm	7.65 lb	6.4 lb
Munich malt	1,500 gm	1,350 gm	2.95 lb	2.45 lb

START OF BOIL

Northern brewer hops	50 gm	50 gm	1.7 oz	1.4 oz

LAST 15 MINUTES OF BOIL

Irish moss	10 gm	10 gm	.35 oz	.30 oz

BREWING METHOD
Temperature-stepped infusion or single-decoction mash. Bottom-working lager yeast

MASH SCHEDULE	52°C - 25 minutes (126°F)	
	66°C - 60 minutes (151F)	
BOIL TIME	90 minutes	
RACKING GRAVITY	1011	2.7° Plato
ALCOHOL CONTENT	5.0% by volume	4.0% by weight
BITTERNESS	30 EBU	
COLOUR	11 EBC	

Ferment at 10-15°C (50-59°F), lager at 10°C (50°F) for two months

EINBECKER
HELL

German pale bock beer. Rich perfumy hops and tart fruit aromas, spicy hop and fruit in the mouth, bitter-sweet finish becomes dry with good hops and citric fruit.

ORIGINAL GRAVITY	1067		16.3° Plato	

	25 litres	23 litres	5 UK gals	5 US gals
Lager malt (Pilsen)	7,110 gm	6,540 gm	14.2 lb	11.85 lb
Caramunich malt	350 gm	320 gm	11.2 oz	9.3 oz
START OF BOIL				
Hallertau hops	50 gm	45 gm	1.6 oz	1.3 oz
Tettnang hops	20 gm	20 gm	.7 oz	.6 oz
LAST 15 MINUTES OF BOIL				
Irish moss	10 gm	10 gm	.35 oz	.30 oz

BREWING METHOD
Temperature-stepped infusion or double-decoction mash. Bottom-fermenting lager yeast

MASH SCHEDULE	50°C - 30 minutes (122°F)	
	65°C - 60 minutes (149°F)	
	76°C - 5 minutes (169°F) then run-off	
BOIL TIME	90 minutes	
RACKING GRAVITY	1015	3.7° Plato
ALCOHOL CONTENT	7.0% by volume	5.5% by weight
BITTERNESS	38 EBU	
COLOUR	15 EBC	

Einbecker employ a double-decoction mash and mature this beer for eight to ten weeks. The 76°C mashing stage is not really necessary, certainly in the home brewing environment, and can be omitted without penalty. The simple two-temperature mash given in chapter 10 is perfectly satisfactory. Ferment at 10-15°C (50-59°F), mature for two months.

GAMBRINUS
GAMBRINUS

Czech Pilsner. Fresh hop and new-mown grass aroma. Rounded grain and hop in the mouth, dry hoppy finish.

ORIGINAL GRAVITY 1048   11.9° Plato

	25 litres	23 litres	5 UK gals	5 US gals
Lager malt (Pilsen)	4,520 gm	4,160 gm	9.05 lb	7.55 lb
White sucrose	500 gm	465 gm	1.0 lb	13.4 oz

START OF BOIL

	25 litres	23 litres	5 UK gals	5 US gals
Saaz hops	80 gm	70 gm	2.5 oz	2.1 oz

LAST 15 MINUTES OF BOIL

	25 litres	23 litres	5 UK gals	5 US gals
Saaz hops	15 gm	15 gm	.55 oz	.45 oz
Irish moss	10 gm	10 gm	.35 oz	.30 oz

BREWING METHOD
Temperature-stepped infusion or double-decoction mash

MASH SCHEDULE	50°C - 30 minutes (122°F)
	63°C - 60 minutes (145°F)
	70°C - 15 minutes (158°F)
BOIL TIME	90 minutes
RACKING GRAVITY	1008 1.9° Plato
ALCOHOL CONTENT	5.4% by volume 4.3% by weight
BITTERNESS	33 EBU
COLOUR	3 EBC

Ferment at 10-12°C (50-54°F), lager for six weeks

MALT EXTRACT VERSION:
Replace the lager malt with the appropriate quantity of pale coloured malt extract syrup and brew using the instructions given in chapter 8.
25l = 3,450 gm: 23l = 3,200 gm: 5UK = 6.9 lb: 5US = 5.8 lb

GROLSCH
PREMIUM LAGER

Dutch lager beer. Floral hop and delicate fresh-mown grass aromas. Some citric fruit notes in the mouth, gentle bitter-sweet finish with good hop character.

ORIGINAL GRAVITY	1048	11.9° Plato

	25 litres	23 litres	5 UK gals	5 US gals
Lager malt (Pilsen)	4,480 gm	4,130 gm	8.95 lb	7.45 lb
Flaked maize	790 gm	730 gm	1.55 lb	1.3 lb
START OF BOIL				
Saaz hops	30 gm	30 gm	1.0 oz	.9 oz
Hallertau hops	25 gm	20 gm	.8 oz	.6 oz
LAST 15 MINUTES OF BOIL				
Irish moss	10 gm	10 gm	.35 oz	.30 oz

BREWING METHOD
Temperature-stepped infusion or double-decoction mash. Bottom-working lager yeast

MASH SCHEDULE	50°C - 20 minutes (122°F)	
	62°C - 45 minutes (144°F)	
	70°C - 45 minutes (158°F)	
BOIL TIME	90 minutes	
RACKING GRAVITY	1011	2.7° Plato
ALCOHOL CONTENT	5.0% by volume	4.0% by weight
BITTERNESS	27 EBU	
COLOUR	3 EBC	

Lagered for ten weeks

HACKER-PSCHORR
MUNCHENER HELL

German lager. Light malt aroma. Quenching bitter-sweet malt and hops in the mouth, malty finish. A rare example of an exported version of a classic Bavarian everyday beer — the German equivalent of a British running bitter.

ORIGINAL GRAVITY	1046	11.4° Plato	

	25 litres	23 litres	5 UK gals	5 US gals
Lager malt (Pilsen)	5,100 gm	4,700 gm	10.2 lb	8.5 lb

START OF BOIL

Hallertau hops	12 gm	10 gm	.4 oz	.3 oz
Tettnang hops	30 gm	30 gm	1.0 oz	.8 oz

LAST 15 MINUTES OF BOIL

Irish moss	10 gm	10 gm	.35 oz	.30 oz

BREWING METHOD
Temperature-stepped infusion or single-decoction mash. Bottom fermenting yeast

MASH SCHEDULE	50°C - 30 minutes (122°F)	
	66°C - 60 minutes (151°F)	
BOIL TIME	90 minutes	
RACKING GRAVITY	1010	2.6° Plato
ALCOHOL CONTENT	4.8% by volume	3.8% by weight
BITTERNESS	20 EBU	
COLOUR	4 EBC	

Lager for one month

HACKER-PSCHORR
EDELHELL EXPORT

German lager. Rich malt aroma with creamy vanilla notes. Delicate refreshing malt and hop in mouth, light malt finish becoming dry.

ORIGINAL GRAVITY	1052	12.8° Plato

	25 litres	23 litres	5 UK gals	5 US gals
Lager malt (Pilsen)	5,760 gm	5,300 gm	11.5 lb	9.6 lb
START OF BOIL				
Hallertau hops	15 gm	15 gm	.5 oz	.4 oz
Tettnang hops	40 gm	35 gm	1.2 oz	1.0 oz
LAST 15 MINUTES OF BOIL				
Irish moss	10 gm	10 gm	.35 oz	.30 oz

BREWING METHOD
Temperature-stepped infusion or single decoction mash. Bottom fermenting yeast

MASH SCHEDULE	50°C - 30 minutes (122°F)	
	66°C - 60 minutes (151°F)	
BOIL TIME	90 minutes	
RACKING GRAVITY	1012	2.9° Plato
ALCOHOL CONTENT	5.4% by volume	4.2% by weight
BITTERNESS	24 EBU	
COLOUR	4 EBC	

Lagered for two months

JEVER
PILS

German Pilsner-style beer. Rich aromas of malt and hop. Delicate and refreshing balance of malt and hop in the mouth leading into stunningly dry finish with superb blend of hop and honey sweetness.

ORIGINAL GRAVITY	1047	11.6° Plato

	25 litres	23 litres	5 UK gals	5 US gals
Pale malt	4,800 gm	4,400 gm	9.55 lb	7.95 lb
Carapils	480 gm	440 gm	15.2 oz	12.6 oz

START OF BOIL

	25 litres	23 litres	5 UK gals	5 US gals
Hallertau hops	25 gm	25 gm	.9 oz	.7 oz
Tettnang hops	70 gm	60 gm	2.2 oz	1.8 oz

LAST 15 MINUTES OF BOIL

	25 litres	23 litres	5 UK gals	5 US gals
Hallertau hops	20 gm	18 gm	.65 oz	.55 oz
Irish moss	10 gm	10 gm	.35 oz	.30 oz

BREWING METHOD
Simple infusion mash - bottom working yeast

MASH SCHEDULE	66°C - 90 minutes (151°F)	
BOIL TIME	90 minutes	
RACKING GRAVITY	1011	2.6° Plato
ALCOHOL CONTENT	4.9% by volume	3.8% by weight
BITTERNESS	44 EBU	
COLOUR	12 EBC	

Ferment at 10-15°C (50-59°F), lager for 90 days.

MALT EXTRACT VERSION:
Replace the pale malt with the appropriate quantity of pale coloured malt extract syrup and brew using the instructions given in chapter 8. 25l = 3,700 gm: 23l = 3,400 gm: 5UK = 7.4 lb: 5US = 6.1 lb

LÖWENBRÄU
SPECIAL EXPORT

German Pilsner-style beer. Malt, cobnut and lemon aromas.
Delicate refreshing palate, dry malty finish with some hop notes.

ORIGINAL GRAVITY	1052		12.8° Plato	

	25 litres	23 litres	5 UK gals	5 US gals
Pale malt	5,500 gm	5,060 gm	11.0 lb	9.15 lb
Carapils	290 gm	265 gm	9.3 oz	7.7 oz

START OF BOIL

	25 litres	23 litres	5 UK gals	5 US gals
Northern brewer hops	15 gm	10 gm	.4 oz	.4 oz
Hallertau hops	15 gm	15 gm	.5 oz	.4 oz
Tettnang hops	20 gm	15 gm	.6 oz	.5 oz

LAST 15 MINUTES OF BOIL

	25 litres	23 litres	5 UK gals	5 US gals
Irish moss	10 gm	10 gm	.35 oz	.30 oz

BREWING METHOD
Temperature-stepped infusion or double-decoction mash. Bottom-fermenting lager yeast

MASH SCHEDULE	50°C - 30 minutes (122°F)	
	62°C - 40 minutes (144°F)	
	72°C - 40 minutes (162°F)	
BOIL TIME	90 minutes	
RACKING GRAVITY	1012	2.9° Plato
ALCOHOL CONTENT	5.4% by volume	4.2% by weight
BITTERNESS	24 EBU	
COLOUR	11 EBC	

Lager for five weeks.

MALT EXTRACT VERSION:
Replace the pale malt with the appropriate quantity of pale coloured malt extract syrup and brew using the instructions given in chapter 8. 25l = 4,200 gm: 23l = 3,900 gm: 5UK = 8.4 lb: 5US = 7.0 lb

METEOR
METEOR PILS

French lager. Toasty grain and hop aromas. Delicate grain and hop in the mouth, dry finish with good hop character and honey notes.

ORIGINAL GRAVITY	1050		12.3° Plato	

	25 litres	**23 litres**	**5 UK gals**	**5 US gals**
Lager malt (Pilsen)	4,670 gm	4,300 gm	9.35 lb	7.75 lb
Flaked maize	820 gm	760 gm	1.65 lb	1.35 lb

START OF BOIL				
Saaz hops	85 gm	75 gm	2.7 oz	2.2 oz

LAST 15 MINUTES OF BOIL				
Irish moss	10 gm	10 gm	.35 oz	.30 oz

BREWING METHOD
Temperature stepped infusion or single decoction mash. Bottom fermenting yeast

MASH SCHEDULE	50°C - 30 minutes (122°F)	
	66°C - 60 minutes (151°F)	
BOIL TIME	90 minutes	
RACKING GRAVITY	1011	2.8° Plato
ALCOHOL CONTENT	5.2% by volume	4.1% by weight
BITTERNESS	35 EBU	
COLOUR	4 EBC	

Lagered for one month

MOUSEL
MOUSEL PREMIUM PILS

Luxembourg lager. Rich malt aroma with hop notes developing. Delicate malt and hop in the mouth, light hoppy finish.

ORIGINAL GRAVITY   1046   11.4° Plato

	25 litres	23 litres	5 UK gals	5 US gals
Lager malt (Pilsen)	4,560 gm	4,200 gm	9.1 lb	7.6 lb
Flaked rice	510 gm	465 gm	1.0 lb	13.5 oz
START OF BOIL				
Saaz hops	45 gm	45 gm	1.5 oz	1.2 oz
Hallertau hops	15 gm	10 gm	.5 oz	.4 oz
LAST 15 MINUTES OF BOIL				
Irish moss	10 gm	10 gm	.35 oz	.30 oz

BREWING METHOD
Temperature-stepped infusion or double-decoction mash. Bottom-working yeast

MASH SCHEDULE	50°C - 30 minutes (122°F)	
	62°C - 30 minutes (144°F)	
BOIL TIME	90 minutes	
RACKING GRAVITY	1010	2.6° Plato
ALCOHOL CONTENT	4.8% by volume	3.8% by weight
BITTERNESS	28 EBU	
COLOUR	3 EBC	

Flaked rice is available through the home brew trade and can be added directly to the mash tun. Alternatively, use domestic rice and boil it in a minimal amount of water for half an hour before adding it to the mash tun, water and all. This beer is lagered for five weeks

PLZEN
PILSNER URQUELL

Czech Pilsner lager. Enormous bouquet of malt and hop flowers.
Complex, multi-layered balance of malt, vanilla, hop. Deep
finish with fruit, hops and spices.

ORIGINAL GRAVITY 1048 11.9° Plato

	25 litres	23 litres	5 UK gals	5 US gals
Lager malt (Pilsen)	5,080 gm	4,670 gm	10.15 lb	8.45 lb
Carapils	265 gm	245 gm	8.6 oz	7.1 oz
START OF BOIL				
Saaz hops	75 gm	70 gm	2.3 oz	1.9 oz
LAST 45 MINUTES OF BOIL				
Saaz hops	35 gm	35 gm	1.2 oz	1.0 oz
LAST 15 MINUTES OF BOIL				
Saaz hops	15 gm	15 gm	.55 gm	.45 gm
Irish moss	10 gm	10 gm	.35 oz	.30 oz

BREWING METHOD
Temperature-stepped infusion or triple-decoction mash. Bottom-
working lager yeast

MASH SCHEDULE	50°C - 20 minutes (122°F)
	60°C - 20 minutes (140°F)
	65°C - 30 minutes (149°F)
	70°C - 20 minutes (158°F)
BOIL TIME	150 minutes (see below)
RACKING GRAVITY	1011 2.7° Plato
ALCOHOL CONTENT	5.0% by volume 4.0% by weight
BITTERNESS	40 EBU
COLOUR	6 EBC

The commercial version of this beer is simmered for two-and-a-half
to three hours, rather than being boiled hard for 60-90 minutes. The
Burton brewers used also to do this during the nineteenth century.
According to one contemporary writer, this gave the Burton beers
their soft, agreeable bitterness. This beer is, apparently, fermented at
the relatively low temperature of 6°C (43°F) and lagered for about
ten weeks at 1°C (35°F).

Dark lagers and Bock beers

DARK LAGERS, BOCKS, DOUBLE-BOCKS,

TRIPLE-BOCKS, OKTOBERFEST MÄRZEN

In common with the dark mild ales of Britain, dark lager – Dunkel – remained the most popular style of beer in Bavaria until the 1950s. Brown beers had dominated brewing in the German-speaking areas for centuries, both the result of kilning malt over wood fires and the hijacking of wheat for brewing by the aristocracy. When the world-famous Reinheitsgebot was drawn up in 1516 by the Bavarian royal family there was no mention of wheat. Beer, it was stipulated, could be brewed only from malted barley, water, hops and yeast. Wheat was excluded because paler wheat beer was considered a speciality that could be appreciated only by those with refined tastes. Even when wheat beer was licensed by the royals to commercial brewers in the 19th century and became widely available, brown beers remained the dominant style. When Gabriel Sedlmayr started his experiments with cold fermentation in Munich in the 1830s, his first lager beers were brown, due partly to consumer preference and partly to the cost of pale malts kilned over expensive coal fires and needing double or triple decoction as a result of high levels of protein.

The first pale lager was not brewed by Sedlmayr's Spaten Brewery until 1894, an astonishing 50 years after the first golden lager had appeared in Pilsen. Pale lagers did not begin to capture a sizeable part of the market until the 1920s. Dark lager today is a small but important part of the beer market. The dunkel brewed by Crown Prince Luitpold of Kaltenberg is regarded as a classic of the style, which is ironic considering it was his predecessors who considered it demeaning to drink beer made from dark malted barley. The fascination of the style lies in the use of dark malt with pale, a well-kilned type known as Munich malt, which avoids the bitter chocolate or roasted character of British dark malts. Munich dark imparts a sweeter, fruity character with light hints of smooth chocolate or cappuccino coffee, balanced by aromatic Hallertau hops.

The French beer listed below, Bière de Paris, although now brewed in Douai, is an ancient style developed in the French capital centuries ago when it was the convention to store brown beers in icy caves by the River Seine. The cold encouraged the yeast to fall to the bottom of the conditioning vessels, an early form of empirical lagering.

Though it is fiercely contested in Bavaria, the origins of the beer style known as Bock lie in the Saxon town of Einbeck to the north. Strong beer, almost certainly top-fermenting at first, has been brewed in the town near Hanover and Brunswick since at least 1351. The fame of the beers led to their being known simply as Beck and this was corrupted to Bock in the Bavarian dialect. Bock also means a billy goat and this symbol of strength and virility is widely used on Bock beer labels in both Germany and the Netherlands. The reason for the popularity of Bocks in Bavaria is due to the marriage of a duke of Brunswick and the daughter of a Bavarian aristocrat in the 17th century. The Bavarians took the style to their hearts, refashioned them to suit their own tastes and later brewed them by bottom fermentation. In earlier times they became closely identified with monasteries where Double Bock beers were brewed for the Lent period of fasting; the beers, known as 'liquid bread', were a vital part of the monks' diet. The most famous Bavarian Double Bock is Paulaner's Salvator. The brewery was founded by monks and Salvator means Holy Father. Many other brewers produce a Double Bock with -or in the title. Bocks may be pale as well as brown but they are high in alcohol, firm bodied and malty, though the pale Maibocks brewed for the spring tend to have a richer hop character.

The Bavarian style known as Märzen — March beer — is under threat. The beer was brewed in March then stored until the autumn and tapped at the start of the Oktoberfest. It is a rich, rounded malty brew with gentle hoppiness. But commercial pressure to reduce long lagering that uses up conditioning vessels has seen Märzen replaced by Oktoberfest beers that are more conventional modern lagers with much shorter conditioning times.

AYINGER
ALTBARISH DUNKEL

German dark lager. Spicy hop and dark fruit aroma, rich, dark fruit in the mouth, big hop and tart fruit finish.

ORIGINAL GRAVITY	1053	13° Plato

	25 litres	23 litres	5 UK gals	5 US gals
Munich malt (dark)	5,560 gm	5,120 gm	11.1 lb	9.25 lb
Caramunich malt	345 gm	315 gm	11.0 oz	9.1 oz
START OF BOIL				
Saaz hops	15 gm	13 gm	.5 oz	.4 oz
Hallertau hops	25 gm	23 gm	.8 oz	.7 oz
LAST 15 MINUTES OF BOIL				
Irish moss	10 gm	10 gm	.35 oz	.30 oz

BREWING METHOD
Temperature-stepped infusion or double-decoction mash. Bottom-fermenting yeast

MASH SCHEDULE	50°C - 30 minutes (122°F)	
	66°C - 60 minutes (151°F)	
BOIL TIME	90 minutes	
RACKING GRAVITY	1012	2.9° Plato
ALCOHOL CONTENT	5.5% by volume	4.3% by weight
BITTERNESS	21 EBU	
COLOUR	52 EBC	

Ferment at 10-15°C (50-59°F), mature for six weeks.

BRAND
IMPERATOR

Dutch dark double-bock lager. Rich malt aroma with a touch of vanilla. Creamy and slightly sweet with a delicate hop finish. An amber bock beer that has a rounded character, from the Brand Brewery, Wijlre, Holland's oldest surviving brewery.

ORIGINAL GRAVITY   1072   17.4° Plato

	25 litres	23 litres	5 UK gals	5 US gals
Pale malt	5,900 gm	5,400 gm	11.75 lb	9.8 lb
Munich malt (light)	2,000 gm	1850 gm	4.0 lb	3.3 lb
Chocolate malt	100 gm	90 gm	3.2 oz	2.6 oz

START OF BOIL

Northern brewer hops	20 gm	15 gm	.6 oz	.5 oz
Hersbrucker hops	20 gm	15 gm	.6 oz	.5 oz

LAST 15 MINUTES OF BOIL

Hersbrucker hops	15 gm	15 gm	.50 oz	.40 oz
Irish moss	10 gm	10 gm	.35 oz	.30 oz

BREWING METHOD
Temperature-stepped infusion mash. Bottom-working lager yeast

MASH SCHEDULE	50°C - 30 minutes (122°F)	
	65°C - 60 minutes (149°F)	
BOIL TIME	90 minutes	
RACKING GRAVITY	1017	4.0° Plato
ALCOHOL CONTENT	7.4% by volume	5.8% by weight
BITTERNESS	22 EBU	
COLOUR	50 EBC	

Lager for six to eight weeks

EGGENBERG
URBOCK 23

Austrian strong red triple-bock beer. Ripe fruity aroma with powerful dash of hop. Rounded balance of grain and hop with a long hoppy finish. A beautifully balanced beer and, because of the long conditioning period, light and refreshing despite the impressive strength.

ORIGINAL GRAVITY	1098	23° Plato	

	25 litres	**23 litres**	**5 UK gals**	**5 US gals**
Lager malt (Pilsen)	6,460 gm	5,950 gm	12.9 lb	10.75 lb
Munich malt (light)	4,400 gm	4,050 gm	8.8 lb	7.3 lb
START OF BOIL				
Saaz hops	50 gm	45 gm	1.5 oz	1.3 oz
Hallertau hops	35 gm	35 gm	1.1 oz	.9 oz
LAST 15 MINUTES OF BOIL				
Saaz hops	15 gm	15 gm	.55 oz	.45 oz
Irish moss	10 gm	10 gm	.35 oz	.30 oz

BREWING METHOD
Temperature-stepped infusion or double-decoction mash. Bottom-fermenting yeast

MASH SCHEDULE	52°C - 20 minutes (126°F)	
	68°C - 60 minutes (154°F)	
BOIL TIME	90 minutes	
RACKING GRAVITY	1022	5.2° Plato
ALCOHOL CONTENT	10.2% by volume	7.9% by weight
BITTERNESS	40 EBU	
COLOUR	25 EBC	

The commercial version of this beer is lagered for nine months.

EINBECKER
DUNKEL

German dark bock beer. Massive fruit, spices and hops aroma, big fruit and hops in the mouth, long finish packed with dark raisin fruit and hops.

ORIGINAL GRAVITY   1067   16.3° Plato

	25 litres	23 litres	5 UK gals	5 US gals
Munich malt (light)	7,200 gm	6,600 gm	14.35 lb	12.0 lb
Caramunich malt	260 gm	240 gm	8.4 oz	7.0 oz

START OF BOIL

Northern brewer hops	15 gm	15 gm	.5 oz	.4 oz
Hersbrucker hops	50 gm	45 gm	1.6 oz	1.3 oz

LAST 15 MINUTES OF BOIL

Irish moss	10 gm	10 gm	.35 oz	.30 oz

BREWING METHOD
Temperature-stepped infusion or single-decoction mash. Bottom-fermenting lager yeast

MASH SCHEDULE	50°C - 30 minutes (122°F)
	65°C - 60 minutes (149°F)
	76°C -5 minutes (169°F) then run-off
BOIL TIME	90 minutes
RACKING GRAVITY	1015 3.7° Plato
ALCOHOL CONTENT	7.0% by volume 5.5% by weight
BITTERNESS	38 EBU
COLOUR	40 EBC

Einbecker use a double-decoction mash, which the mash schedule listed above is designed to imitate. However, the 76°C stage is only to reduce mash viscosity and make run-off easier. It can be omitted if required. Ferment at 10-15°C (50-59°F), mature beer for eight to ten weeks at 5-10°C (41-50°F).

EINBECKER
MAIBOCK

German double-bock beer. Rich fruit and perfumy hop aroma, big attack of raisin and sultana fruit in the mouth, long, complex finish with dark fruit, perfumy hops and ripe malt.

ORIGINAL GRAVITY	1067	16.3° Plato

	25 litres	23 litres	5 UK gals	5 US gals
Lager malt (Pilsen)	4,600 gm	4,250 gm	9.15 lb	7.65 lb
Munich malt (dark)	2,850 gm	2,600 gm	5.65 lb	4.7 lb

START OF BOIL

	25 litres	23 litres	5 UK gals	5 US gals
Northern brewer hops	35 gm	30 gm	1 oz	.8 oz
Hallertau hops	30 gm	30 gm	1 oz	.8 oz

LAST 15 MINUTES OF BOIL

	25 litres	23 litres	5 UK gals	5 US gals
Irish moss	10 gm	10 gm	.35 oz	.30 oz

BREWING METHOD
Temperature-stepped infusion or double-decoction mash. Bottom-fermenting lager yeast

MASH SCHEDULE	50°C - 30 minutes (122°F)
	65°C - 60 minutes (149°F)
	76°C - 5 minutes (169°F) then run-off
BOIL TIME	90 minutes
RACKING GRAVITY	1015 3.7° Plato
ALCOHOL CONTENT	7.0% by volume 5.5% by weight
BITTERNESS	36 EBU
COLOUR	25 EBC

This is Einbecker's seasonal beer, sold during the month of May, Einbecker apparently use a double-decoction mash and mature Maibock for around six weeks. The 76°C mashing stage is not necessary and can be omitted if desired.

EKU
KULMINATOR

German dark double-bock beer. Roasted grain and spicy hop aroma, dark malt and tart fruit in the mouth, long, complex finish with massive fruit, spices and hops.

ORIGINAL GRAVITY	1077		18.5° Plato	

	25 litres	23 litres	5 UK gals	5 US gals
Munich malt (light)	7,920 gm	7,290 gm	15.85 lb	13.2 lb
Roasted caramalt	680 gm	620 gm	1.35 lb	1.1 lb

START OF BOIL

Northern brewer hops	40 gm	38 gm	1.3 oz	1.1 oz

LAST 15 MINUTES OF BOIL

Irish moss	10 gm	10 gm	.35 oz	.30 oz

BREWING METHOD
Temperature-stepped infusion or single decoction mash. Bottom fermenting lager yeast

MASH SCHEDULE	50°C - 30 minutes (122°F)	
	67°C - 60 minutes (153°F)	
BOIL TIME	90 minutes	
RACKING GRAVITY	1017	4.2° Plato
ALCOHOL CONTENT	8.0% by volume	6.3% by weight
BITTERNESS	24 EBU	
COLOUR	65 EBC	

HACKER-PSCHORR
OKTOBERFEST MARZEN

Munich Oktoberfest Märzen. Rich hop aroma with gentle resiny hop character. Creamy grain in the mouth, deep dry finish, with biscuity malt and peppery hop.

ORIGINAL GRAVITY 1055   13.5° Plato

	25 litres	23 litres	5 UK gals	5 US gals
Lager malt (Pilsen)	3,140 gm	2,880 gm	6.25 lb	5.2 lb
Munich malt (dark)	2,960 gm	2,720 gm	5.9 lb	4.9 lb

START OF BOIL

	25 litres	23 litres	5 UK gals	5 US gals
Hallertau hops	21 gm	20 gm	.7 oz	.6 oz
Tettnang hops	29 gm	27 gm	1.0 oz	.8 oz

LAST 15 MINUTES OF BOIL

	25 litres	23 litres	5 UK gals	5 US gals
Irish moss	10 gm	10 gm	.35 oz	.30 oz

BREWING METHOD
Temperature-stepped infusion or double-decoction mash. Bottom-fermenting yeast

MASH SCHEDULE	50°C - 30 minutes (122°F)	
	66°C - 60 minutes (151°F)	
BOIL TIME	90 minutes	
RACKING GRAVITY	1012	3.0° Plato
ALCOHOL CONTENT	5.7% by volume	4.5% by weight
BITTERNESS	25 EBU	
COLOUR	25 EBC	

Lagered for two months

KALTENBERG
KONIG LUDWIG DUNKEL

*German dark lager. Malt and chocolate aroma. Light, refreshing
malt in the mouth, dry finish with some coffee notes.*

ORIGINAL GRAVITY 1055 13.5° Plato

	25 litres	23 litres	5 UK gals	5 US gals
Pale malt	5,900 gm	5,450 gm	11.8 lb	9.85 lb
Chocolate malt	200 gm	190 gm	6.6 oz	5.5 oz

START OF BOIL

Hallertau hops	45 gm	40 gm	1.4 oz	1.2 oz

LAST 15 MINUTES OF BOIL

Hallertau hops	10 gm	10 gm	.35 oz	.30 oz
Irish moss	10 gm	10 gm	.35 oz	.30 oz

BREWING METHOD
Temperature-stepped infusion or triple-decoction mash. Bottom-
fermenting yeast

MASH SCHEDULE	52°C - 20 minutes (122°F)	
	62°C - 30 minutes (140°F)	
	68°C - 30 minutes (154°F)	
	72°C - 10 minutes (162°F)	
BOIL TIME	90 minutes	
RACKING GRAVITY	1013	3.3° Plato
ALCOHOL CONTENT	5.6% by volume	4.4% by weight
BITTERNESS	25 EBU	
COLOUR	75 EBC	

MALT EXTRACT VERSION:
Replace the pale malt with the appropriate quantity of pale coloured
malt extract syrup and brew using the instructions given in chapter 8.
25l = 4,500 gm: 23l = 4,160 gm: 5UK = 9.1 lb: 5US = 7.5 lb

LUTÈCE
BIÈRE DE PARIS

French dark lager. Malt and fruit aromas. Malt, raisin fruit in the mouth, deep finish with liquorice and chocolate notes.

ORIGINAL GRAVITY	1063	15.3° Plato

	25 litres	23 litres	5 UK gals	5 US gals
Munich malt (light)	3,140 gm	2,890 gm	6.25 lb	5.2 lb
Lager malt (Pilsen)	2,990 gm	2,750 gm	5.95 lb	4.95 lb
Crystal malt	540 gm	495 gm	1.05 lb	14.3 oz
Amber malt	390 gm	360 gm	12.5 oz	10.4 oz
START OF BOIL				
Saaz hops	55 gm	50 gm	1.8 oz	1.5 oz
LAST 15 MINUTES OF BOIL				
Irish moss	10 gm	10 gm	.35 oz	.30 oz

BREWING METHOD
Temperature-stepped infusion or double-decoction mash. Bottom-fermenting yeast

MASH SCHEDULE	50°C - 30 minutes (122°F)	
	66°C - 60 minutes (151°F)	
BOIL TIME	90 minutes	
RACKING GRAVITY	1014	3.5° Plato
ALCOHOL CONTENT	6.6% by volume	5.3% by weight
BITTERNESS	23 EBU	
COLOUR	50 EBC	

PAULANER
SALVATOR DOUBLE BOCK

*German dark double-bock beer. Spicy fruit and hops aroma,
rich, dark malt and fruit in the mouth, long finish packed with
dark sultana fruit and spicy hop.*

ORIGINAL GRAVITY 1072   17.4° Plato

	25 litres	23 litres	5 UK gals	5 US gals
Munich malt (light)	4,600 gm	4,200 gm	9.15 lb	7.6 lb
Munich malt (dark)	2,800 gm	2,600 gm	5.6 lb	4.65 lb
Caramunich malt	650 gm	600 gm	1.25 lb	1.05 lb

START OF BOIL

Hallertau hops	55 gm	50 gm	1.7 oz	1.4 oz

LAST 15 MINUTES OF BOIL

Irish moss	10 gm	10 gm	.35 oz	.30 oz

BREWING METHOD
Temperature-stepped infusion or double-decoction mash. Bottom-
fermenting yeast

MASH SCHEDULE	50°C - 30 minutes (122°F)
	66°C - 60 minutes (151°F)
BOIL TIME	90 minutes
RACKING GRAVITY	1016 3.9° Plato
ALCOHOL CONTENT	7.5% by volume 5.9% by weight
BITTERNESS	30 EBU
COLOUR	60 EBC

SPATEN
OKTOBERFEST MÄRZEN

Munich Oktoberfest bier. Pale copper-coloured beer with tart fruit, vanilla and hops on the nose, big, mouth-filling malt and hops; perfumy hops and rich malt dominate the finish.

ORIGINAL GRAVITY	1055		13.5° Plato	

	25 litres	23 litres	5 UK gals	5 US gals
Vienna malt	3,210 gm	2,950 gm	6.4 lb	5.35 lb
Munich malt (dark)	2,710 gm	2,500 gm	5.4 lb	4.5 lb
Caramunich malt	235 gm	220 gm	7.6 oz	6.3 oz

START OF BOIL				
Hallertau hops	37 gm	34 gm	1.2 oz	1.0 oz

LAST 15 MINUTES OF BOIL				
Hallertau hops	15 gm	15 gm	.55 oz	.45 oz
Irish moss	10 gm	10 gm	.35 oz	.30 oz

BREWING METHOD
Temperature-stepped infusion or double-decoction mash. Bottom-fermenting yeast

MASH SCHEDULE	50°C - 30 minutes (122°F)	
	66°C - 60 minutes (151°F)	
BOIL TIME	90 minutes	
RACKING GRAVITY	1012	3.0° Plato
ALCOHOL CONTENT	5.7% by volume	4.5% by weight
BITTERNESS	22 EBU	
COLOUR	32 EBC	

Lagered for two months

Esoteric beers

WHEAT BEERS, FRUIT BEERS, SPICED

BEERS, SMOKED BEERS, SOURED ALES

The beers in this chapter are of special interest for they represent ancient styles of brewing that became almost hidden from view by the surge of modern lagers. They have been saved and revived by the renewed interest in historic styles. As was explained in the previous chapter, Bavarian wheat beers were once the 'house beers' of the monarchy and aristocracy. When they became available commercially in the 19th century they were quickly challenged in popularity by the new lager beers. By the 1970s wheat beers had been reduced to a sideline, dismissed as 'old ladies' beers'. But in the 1980s wheat beer enjoyed an astonishing boom that has taken it to 30 per cent of the market. At the Spaten Brewery, where bottom-fermenting lagers were first developed, its Franziskaner wheat beers now account for half its production. Wheat beers are members of the ale family. In spite of the name, they are made from a blend of malted barley and malted wheat (barley malt contains more enzymes than wheat malt and also has a husk that acts as a filter during mashing). Hops are used sparingly, more for their preservative power than for bitterness, as bitterness does not blend well with the fruitiness created by fermentation. The typical aromas of Bavarian wheat beers are apples, cloves, and banana.

The wheat beers of Berlin are in sad decline, with just two producers left. They are low in alcohol, around 2.5 to three per cent, with a low hop rate. After mashing and boiling, lactic cultures as well as a top-fermenting yeast strain are added, with the result that the beer has a tart and sour aroma and flavour. Many drinkers add a dash of woodruff or other sweet syrups to balance the tartness of the beer.

Belgian wheat or 'white' beers are also much in vogue. They are also top-fermenting and lightly hopped in order to best express the tart fruitiness of the blend of malted barley and unmalted wheat. The classic Belgian 'white', Hoegaarden, also uses coriander and Curaçao orange peel in the copper; when Belgium was part of the Netherlands, Dutch traders brought spices back from the East Indies, many of which were used by brewers to add depth of flavour and aroma to their beers.

The lambic, gueuze and fruit beers of Belgium are the oldest-surviving beer style still in production. They have been brewed in the Senne Valley region around Brussels for 400 years or more, seemed destined to disappear but are now growing in appreciation again. As lambic is protected by Belgian law, it must be brewed to certain conventions, one of which is that the mash is a blend of barley malt and unmalted wheat, of which wheat must constitute 30 per cent of the grist. Hops are used generously but are deliberately aged for four years to lose their bitterness. After the boil, the hopped wort is pumped to a shallow open vessel called a cool ship in the roof of the brewery. Louvred windows are left open and tiles are removed from the roof to encourage wild air-borne yeasts to enter and attack the malt sugars. When fermentation is under way, the liquid is pumped to large wooden casks in cool, dark cellars. Fermentation and conditioning continue with the aid of micro-organisms in the casks and the cellars. Lambic is the straight beer from the casks, aged for several years. Gueuze, the most popular version, is a blend of young and old lambics. Kriek is cherry beer; bitter cherries have their skins broken and are added to the casks and start a further fermentation. Frambozen or framboise is raspberry beer.

The sour red beers of Flanders were probably inspired by early English porters. Using Vienna malt, similar to English crystal malt, beers such as Rodenbach are mashed and boiled conventionally but are then stored in unlined oak tuns where micro-organisms add a sour and lactic flavour. Rodenbach comes in a young version and Grand Cru, which is a blend of young and aged beers.

The smoked beers of Bamberg in northern Bavaria are another link with brewing's past. Malt is smoked over beechwood fires and the finished brown beer has a delectable smoky aroma and palate. The beer style is one of the oldest known lagers; for centuries before refrigeration, the beers were stored in icy caves in the hills around Bamberg. The new style of whisky malt beers is both an attempt to recreate the ancient style of smoked beers and to cash in on the craze for Scotch whisky in mainland Europe.

ACHOUFFE
LA CHOUFFE

Belgian spiced beer. Spicy, estery with a powerful hop resin aroma. rich balance of malt, spice, and hop in the mouth, intense bitter finish.

ORIGINAL GRAVITY	1080	19.2° Plato

	25 litres	23 litres	5 UK gals	5 US gals
Lager malt (Pilsen)	7,400 gm	6,810 gm	14.8 lb	12.35 lb
Crystal malt	425 gm	390 gm	13.6 oz	11.3 oz
White sucrose	680 gm	630 gm	1.35 lb	1.1 lb
START OF BOIL				
Golding hops	26 gm	23 gm	.8 oz	.7 oz
Styrian Goldings hops	16 gm	15 gm	.5 oz	.5 oz
Saaz hops	25 gm	23 gm	.8 oz	.7 oz
LAST 15 MINUTES OF BOIL				
Irish moss	10 gm	10 gm	.35 oz	.30 oz
Ground coriander seed	5 gm	5 gm	.17 oz	.15 oz
Ground cumin seed	5 gm	5 gm	.17 oz	.15 oz
Ground caraway seed	3 gm	3 gm	.1 oz	.08 oz

BREWING METHOD
Temperature-stepped infusion mash; top-working yeast

MASH SCHEDULE	50°C - 30 minutes (122°F)	
	65°C - 60 minutes (149°F)	
BOIL TIME	90 minutes	
RACKING GRAVITY	1014	3.3° Plato
ALCOHOL CONTENT	8.9% by volume	7.0% by weight
BITTERNESS	30 EBU	
COLOUR	25 EBC	

If the seed is purchased whole it can be ground in a mortar and pestle. Such small quantities tend to get lost in domestic coffee grinders and the like.

MALT EXTRACT VERSION:
Replace the Pilsner malt with the appropriate quantity of pale coloured malt extract syrup and brew using the instructions given in chapter 8.
25l = 5,700 gm: 23l = 5,200 gm: 5UK = 11.4 lb: 5US = 9.5 lb

ADELSHOFFEN
ADELSCOTT BIÈRE AU MALT A WHISKY

French peat-smoked whisky-malt beer. Delectable smoked malt aroma. Rich malt in the mouth, light smoky finish. From the Grande Brasserie Alsacienne d'Adelshoffen, France.

ORIGINAL GRAVITY 1065   15.8° Plato

	25 litres	23 litres	5 UK gals	5 US gals
Peated whisky malt	6,000 gm	5,400 gm	11.85 lb	9.85 lb
Flaked maize	1,350 gm	1,220 gm	2.65 lb	2.2 lb
START OF BOIL				
Styrian Golding hops	15 gm	15 gm	.5 oz	.5 oz
Hallertau hops	15 gm	10 gm	.5 oz	.4 oz
LAST 15 MINUTES OF BOIL				
Irish moss	10 gm	10 gm	.35 oz	.30 oz

BREWING METHOD
Temperature stepped mash - bottom fermenting yeast

MASH SCHEDULE	50°C - 30 minutes (122°C)
	65°C - 60 minutes (149°F)
BOIL TIME	90 minutes
RACKING GRAVITY	1015 3.6° Plato
ALCOHOL CONTENT	6.8% by volume 5.3% by weight
BITTERNESS	18 EBU
COLOUR	18 EBC

At the time of writing, peated whisky malt is not available through the established home-brew trade in the UK, although one wholesaler has promised to stock it if there is demand. An alternative would be to use Bamberg Rauchmalt, which is available. This is beechwood smoked rather than peat smoked, but it would nevertheless make an interesting beer with a smoky character. If Bamberger Rauchmalt is used, the 50°C mashing stage could probably be dispensed with. A simple infusion mash at 65°C for 60-90 minutes would suffice. ferment as an ale at 18-22°C (50-59°F), condition for six to eight weeks at 13-15°C.

AYINGER
BRAU WEISSE

*German wheat beer. Enticing estery aroma with hints of apple
and cloves. Tart in the mouth with a deep refreshing finish and
lingering fruit notes. A superb wheat beer, pale in colour and
with a spritzy Champagne sparkle in the glass and mouth. From
Brauerei Inselkammer, Aying, Germany.*

ORIGINAL GRAVITY	1049	12.1° Plato

	25 litres	23 litres	5 UK gals	5 US gals
Pale malt	3,100 gm	2,800 gm	6.1 lb	5.1 lb
Wheat malt	2,500 gm	2,300 gm	5.0 lb	4.15 lb

START OF BOIL

	25 litres	23 litres	5 UK gals	5 US gals
Hallertau hops	25 gm	25 gm	.8 oz	.7 oz

BREWING METHOD
Single infusion mash — top fermented

MASH SCHEDULE	65°C - 90 minutes (149°F)	
BOIL TIME	90 minutes	
RACKING GRAVITY	1011	2.7° Plato
ALCOHOL CONTENT	5.1% by volume	4.1% by weight
BITTERNESS	15 EBU	
COLOUR	8 EBC	

Ferment as an ale at 18-22°C (50-59°F) using a good quality real ale
yeast.

CANTILLON
LAMBIC & GUEUZE

Belgian speciality beers. Sour and cidery aroma, sour fruit and hint of nuts in the mouth, mouth-puckeringly dry and tart finish. Lambic is served still, gueuze is less sour, with a spritzy, lively aroma and palate.

ORIGINAL GRAVITY	1052	12.8° Plato

	25 litres	23 litres	5 UK gals	5 US gals
Pale malt	3,800 gm	3,500 gm	7.65 lb	6.35 lb
Cracked raw wheat	2,100 gm	1,900 gm	4.1 lb	3.4 lb

START OF BOIL

	25 litres	23 litres	5 UK gals	5 US gals
Golding hops	40 gm	35 gm	1.2 oz	1.0 oz

BREWING METHOD
Temperature-stepped infusion mash. Top-fermenting yeast

MASH SCHEDULE	45°C - 10 minutes (113°F)	
	58°C - 10 minutes (136°F)	
	65°C - 35 minutes (149°F)	
	72°C - 20 minutes (162°F)	
BOIL TIME	Up to 3 hours	
RACKING GRAVITY	1012	2.9° Plato
ALCOHOL CONTENT	5.4% by volume	4.2% by weight
BITTERNESS	15 EBU	
COLOUR	9 EBC	

Lambic is aged for up to three years in oak casks, during which time wild micro-organisms acidify and sour the beer. Gueuze is a blend of old and young (not so sour) lambic which removes some of the tartness. The complex mash schedule used by many Lambic brewers is probably a bit of an overkill, considering the simple grist, and is probably a matter of tradition. Lambic-style beers are usually regarded as being spontaneously fermented, that is, fermentation occurs naturally by picking up wild micro-organisms from the surrounding air. Some Lambic producers pitch their beers with a top-working yeast for primary fermentation and allow the wild micro-organisms to sour the beer during maturation. The wild micro-organisms that produce the souring are picked up from the open coolers within the brewery and the souring takes place in oak casks during maturation. See the article on sour beers in the appendices.

EGGENBERG
MACQUEENS NESSIE WHISKY MALT BEER

Austrian whisky-malt smoked red beer. Rich malt aroma with delicate hop notes. Powerful grain taste with a long smoky finish — like a whisky and soda according to the brewer. It has a fine amber colour. From the Eggenberg Brewery, Austria.

ORIGINAL GRAVITY	1070	16.9° Plato

	25 litres	23 litres	5 UK gals	5 US gals
Peated whisky malt	7,800 gm	7,200 gm	15.6 lb	13.8 lb
Crystal malt	135 gm	125 gm	4.4 oz	3.7 oz

START OF BOIL

Hallertau hops	45 gm	40 gm	1.5 oz	1.2 oz

LAST 15 MINUTES OF BOIL

Irish moss	10 gm	10 gm	.35 oz	.30 oz

BREWING METHOD
Temperature stepped infusion mash - bottom fermented

MASH SCHEDULE	50°C - 30 minutes (122°F)	
	65°C - 60 minutes (149°F)	
BOIL TIME	90 minutes	
RACKING GRAVITY	1016	3.8° Plato
ALCOHOL CONTENT	7.3% by volume	5.7% by weight
BITTERNESS	27 EBU	
COLOUR	30 EBC	

At the time of writing, peated whisky malt is not available through the established home-brew trade in the UK, although one wholesaler has promised to stock it if there is demand. An alternative would be to use Bamberg Rauchmalt, which is available. This is beechwood smoked rather than peat smoked, but it would nevertheless make an interesting beer with a smoky character. If Bamberger Rauchmalt is used, the 50°C mashing stage could probably be dispensed with. A simple infusion mash at 65°C for 60-90 minutes would suffice. Mature for six months

ERDINGER
HEFE WEISSBIER

Bavarian Weizenbier. Superb apple and cloves aroma. Refreshing grain and tart fruit in the mouth. A classic wheat beer recalling the days of German brewing before modern lagering.

ORIGINAL GRAVITY 1051   12.6° Plato

	25 litres	23 litres	5 UK gals	5 US gals
Wheat malt	3,210 gm	2,950 gm	6.4 lb	5.35 lb
Pale malt	2,630 gm	2,420 gm	5.25 lb	4.35 lb
START OF BOIL				
Tettnang hops	20 gm	18 gm	.65 oz	.55 oz
Perle hops	15 gm	12 gm	.45 oz	.40 oz
HALF WAY THROUGH BOIL (45 MINUTES)				
Tettnang hops	10 gm	10 gm	.35 oz	.30 oz
LAST 15 MINUTES OF BOIL				
Tettnang hops	10 gm	10 gm	.35 oz	.30 oz

BREWING METHOD
Single infusion mash - top working yeast

MASH SCHEDULE	66°C - 90 minutes (151°F)
BOIL TIME	90 minutes
RACKING GRAVITY	1011 2.8° Plato
ALCOHOL CONTENT	5.3% by volume 4.3% by weight
BITTERNESS	18 EBU
COLOUR	9 EBC

Erding apparently use the double decoction mash for this beer, but considering the ingredients, a simple, single-temperature, infusion mash should give good results. Alternatively, a temperature stepped mash giving 30 minutes at 50°C followed by 60 minutes at 66°C, will be a bit more authentic. Ferment at 18-22°C (64-72°F), condition for two to four weeks at 15°C (59°F).

GROLSCH
AMBER

Dutch Ale. A Dutch version of German Alt; a copper-coloured ale with a rich fruit and perfumy hop aroma, cobnuts and hops in the mouth, gentle fruit and hops finish.

ORIGINAL GRAVITY   1048   11.9° Plato

	25 litres	23 litres	5 UK gals	5 US gals
Pale malt	3,860 gm	3,560 gm	7.7 lb	6.45 lb
Wheat malt	1,030 gm	950 gm	2.05 lb	1.7 lb
Crystal malt	540 gm	495 gm	1.05 lb	14.3 oz
START OF BOIL				
Saaz hops	38 gm	35 gm	1.2 oz	1.0 oz
Hallertau hops	42 gm	38 gm	1.3 oz	1.1 oz
LAST 15 MINUTES OF BOIL				
Hallertau hops	15 gm	15 gm	.5 oz	.5 oz
Irish moss	10 gm	10 gm	.35 oz	.30 oz

BREWING METHOD
Single infusion mash - top fermented

MASH SCHEDULE	65°C - 90 minutes (149°F)	
BOIL TIME	90 minutes	
RACKING GRAVITY	1011	2.7° Plato
ALCOHOL CONTENT	5.0% by volume	4.0% by weight
BITTERNESS	40 EBU	
COLOUR	32 EBC	

Grolsch refer to this beer as an amber ale, Michael Jackson regards it as an altbier, but as it has a fairly high percentage of wheat in its make-up I have chosen to classify it along with the other wheat beers.

HOEGAARDEN
WHITE

Belgian spiced wheat beer. Cloudy yellowish classic beer with great spice character, recalling the age before hops were used and spices were added to give bitterness to beer. Spicy aroma with strong coriander notes. Orange and coriander in the mouth, light, dry finish.

ORIGINAL GRAVITY	1048	11.9° Plato

	25 litres	23 litres	5 UK gals	5 US gals
Pale malt	2,800 gm	2,570 gm	5.6 lb	4.65 lb
Unmalted wheat	2,520 gm	2,320 gm	5.0 lb	4.2 lb
Flaked oats	280 gm	255 gm	9.0 oz	7.5 oz
START OF BOIL				
Golding hops	26 gm	24 gm	.9 oz	.7 oz
Saaz hops	17 gm	15 gm	.6 oz	.5 oz
LAST 15 MINUTES OF BOIL				
Saaz hops	15 gm	15 gm	.50 oz	.45 oz
Ground coriander seed	3 gm	3 gm	.1 oz	.08 oz
Dried Curaçao orange peel	3 gm	3 gm	.1 oz	.1 oz

BREWING METHOD
Single infusion mash - top fermenting yeast

MASH SCHEDULE	68°C - 90 minutes (154°F)	
BOIL TIME	90 minutes	
RACKING GRAVITY	1011	2.7° Plato
ALCOHOL CONTENT	5.0% by volume	4.0% by weight
BITTERNESS	18 EBU	
COLOUR	8 EBC	

The raw wheat should be cracked or milled before use; it might be a good idea to boil it for a few minutes in a minimum amount of water to ensure complete gelatinisation, although the gelatinisation temperature of wheat is 58-64°C and should occur at normal mash temperatures. The orange peel (and coriander seed if purchased whole) should be milled before adding to the boiler. The best approach is to pulverise it in a mortar and pestle. Ferment as an ale at about 20°C (68°F), mature for one month in cask at 12-15°C and then bottle, priming with a scant half-teaspoonful of cane sugar. Hoegaarden add a bottom working yeast when bottling.

KINDL
WEISSE

Berliner style weisse beer. Sour and tart aroma, extremely sour palate, quenching finish with, cidery fruit. Berliners traditionally add woodruff or a similar sweet syrup to balance the lactic sourness of the beer.

ORIGINAL GRAVITY   1030   7.5° Plato

	25 litres	23 litres	5 UK gals	5 US gals
Pale malt	2,530 gm	2,330 gm	5.05 lb	4.2 lb
Wheat malt	840 gm	780 gm	1.65 lb	1.4 lb

START OF BOIL

	25 litres	23 litres	5 UK gals	5 US gals
Northern brewer hops	25 gm	20 gm	.7 oz	.6 oz

BREWING METHOD
Single infusion mash - top fermenting yeast. Lactobacillus delbruckii inoculation.

MASH SCHEDULE	66°C - 90 minutes
BOIL TIME	15 minutes (yes really!)
RACKING GRAVITY	1007 1.7° Plato
ALCOHOL CONTENT	3.1% by volume 2.5% by weight
BITTERNESS	8 EBU
COLOUR	5 EBC

The surprisingly short fifteen minute boil really is all the Kindl brewery give to this beer; it's hardly long enough to sterilise the wort. I am not really sure of the technical reasoning behind this: it possibly has something to do with leaving protein in the beer to give the souring micro-organisms something to chew on. The very low hop rate and alcohol level are to preserve the lactic acid producing bacteria; the bacteria would be killed by high levels of alcohol and hop alpha-acid. Clive La Pensee, in his Historical Companion to House Brewing, mentions a remarkably similar WEISSBIER that he found in an 1845 German brewing book, but which probably originates from the 1500s or before.

The brewery inoculate the cooled wort in the fermentation vessel with Lactobacillus delbruckii and leave it a few hours before adding the top working yeast. Fermentation takes place at 20-25°C (68-77°F). The commercial beer is filtered and krausened before bottling. See the article in the appendices on soured beers.

LIEFMANS
KRIEKBIER

Belgian cherry beer. Regarded as Belgium's classic cherry beer. Powerful fruit and hop aroma. Strong cherry fruit in the mouth, long sweet and sour finish. From Liefman's brewery, Oudenaarde, Belgium.

ORIGINAL GRAVITY	1052	12.8° Plato

	25 litres	23 litres	5 UK gals	5 US gals
Lager malt (Pilsen)	4,000 gm	3,700 gm	8.05 lb	6.7 lb
Flaked maize	700 gm	650 gm	1.4 lb	1.15 lb
Torrefied barley	700 gm	650 gm	1.4 lb	1.15 lb
Crystal malt	300 gm	275 gm	9.5 oz	7.9 oz
Chocolate malt	135 gm	125 gm	4.3 oz	3.6 oz
START OF BOIL				
Whitbread Golding hops	25 gm	25 gm	.8 oz	.7 oz
Tettnang hops	20 gm	15 gm	.6 oz	.5 oz
LAST 15 MINUTES OF BOIL				
Saaz hops	10 gm	10 gm	.35 oz	.30 oz
Irish moss	10 gm	10 gm	.35 oz	.30 oz

BREWING METHOD
Single infusion mash - top fermented

MASH SCHEDULE	66°C - 90 minutes	
BOIL TIME	90 minutes	
RACKING GRAVITY	1012	3.0° Plato
ALCOHOL CONTENT	5.3% by volume	4.3% by weight
BITTERNESS	20 EBU	
COLOUR	60 EBC	

The standard beer is matured for about four months in cask, then the cask is opened and about 4.5 kilograms of black cherries are added and the beer is matured for a further six to eight weeks before bottling. Black cherries have a higher sugar level than red cherries. The addition of the cherries will increase the alcohol level to about 7 per cent. Similar quantities of red cherries (kirsebier) or raspberries (frambozenbier) can be added, but in both cases the increase in alcohol level will be less. Some manufacturers of fruit beer add their fruit to the copper during the last 15 minutes of the boil to reduce the risk of contamination. Ferment as an ale at 18-22°C (64-72°F).

PINKUS
PINKUS ALT

German wheat altbier. Rich vinous aroma. Ripe malt and slightly tart in the mouth, long fruity and slightly acidic finish. From Pinkus Muller, Munster Germany. The brewery classifies this beer as an alt, but as it contains 40 per cent wheat malt I regard it as more of a wheat beer. They make another beer that they call a weizen (see Pinkus Hefe Weizen).

ORIGINAL GRAVITY	1050	12.3° Plato	

	25 litres	23 litres	5 UK gals	5 US gals
Lager malt (Pilsen)	3,400 gm	3,130 gm	6.8 lb	5.65 lb
Wheat malt	2,270 gm	2,090 gm	4.5 lb	3.75 lb
START OF BOIL				
Hallertau hops	31 gm	28 gm	1.0 oz	.8 oz
LAST 15 MINUTES OF BOIL				
Irish moss	10 gm	10 gm	.35 oz	.30 oz

BREWING METHOD
Temperature-stepped infusion or single-decoction mash.   Top fermenting yeast

MASH SCHEDULE	50°C - 30 minutes (122°F)	
	66°C - 60 minutes (151°F)	
BOIL TIME	90 minutes	
RACKING GRAVITY	1011	2.8° Plato
ALCOHOL CONTENT	5.2% by volume	4.2% by weight
BITTERNESS	18 EBU	
COLOUR	6 EBC	

The brewery uses a single decoction mash, but a temperature-stepped infusion mash will serve just as well. Indeed, considering the ingredients, a simple, single-temperature infusion mash at 66°C for 90 minutes would be perfectly adequate. This beer is matured for six months in maturation tanks along with a lactic-acid bacteria culture. The lactic character of the beer is not very prominent, which probably means that the bacteria does not cope too well with the relatively high hop and alcohol levels for this type of beer.

PINKUS
PINKUS HEFE WEIZEN

German wheat beer. Light fruit aroma. Delicate and refreshing in the mouth, dry fruity finish. Similar to Pinkus Alt, but with a higher proportion of wheat. This beer has a light hop level, and a quenching fruitiness.

ORIGINAL GRAVITY   1050   12.3° Plato

	25 litres	23 litres	5 UK gals	5 US gals
Pale malt	2,300 gm	2,110 gm	4.55 lb	3.8 lb
Wheat malt	3,440 gm	3,170 gm	6.85 lb	5.75 lb

START OF BOIL

Hallertau hops	31 gm	28 gm	1.0 oz	.8 oz

BREWING METHOD
Temperature-stepped infusion or single-decoction mash. Top fermenting yeast

MASH SCHEDULE	50°C - 30 minutes (122°F)
	66°C - 60 minutes (151°F)
BOIL TIME	90 minutes
RACKING GRAVITY	1011 2.8° Plato
ALCOHOL CONTENT	5.2% by volume 4.2% by weight
BITTERNESS	18 EBU
COLOUR	9 EBC

The brewery uses a single-decoction mash, but a temperature-stepped mash is more appropriate these days. Indeed, as with the previous recipe, there is no reason why a simple infusion mash should not be employed — 66°C for 60-90 minutes should be perfectly adequate. This beer is matured for one month. It does not have the slightly lactic character of Pinkus Alt.

RODENBACH
RODENBACH

Belgian soured ale. Powerful sour and fruity aroma. Ripe fruit in the mouth, long bitter and sour finish. This must be the last surviving example of a beer that uses similar brewing techniques to that of old-time London Porter.

ORIGINAL GRAVITY	1048		11.9° Plato	
	25 litres	**23 litres**	**5 UK gals**	**5 US gals**
Pale malt	3,600 gm	3,300 gm	7.2 lb	6.0 lb
Flaked maize	1,050 gm	960 gm	2.05 lb	1.7 lb
Caramunich malt	550 gm	510 gm	1.1 lb	14.7 oz
Chocolate malt	120 gm	115 gm	3.9 oz	3.3 oz

START OF BOIL				
Golding hops	35 gm	30 gm	1.1 oz	.9 oz

BREWING METHOD
Temperature-stepped infusion or double-decoction mash. Top-fermenting yeast

MASH SCHEDULE	52°C - 20 minutes	
	62°C - 40 minutes	
	72°C - 40 minutes	
BOIL TIME	90 minutes	
RACKING GRAVITY	1012	3.0° Plato
ALCOHOL CONTENT	4.8% by volume	3.8% by weight
BITTERNESS	14 EBU	
COLOUR	60 EBC	

Rodenbach claim to use a double-decoction mash, but a simple infusion mash should do just as well; a double-decoction mash seems rather an overkill, considering the ingredients used. The above recipe is brewed and then matured in cask for five or six weeks. It should then be soured by blending in a smaller quantity of Grand Cru (recipe next page) which is a sour beer. The exact blending ratio is part of the brewers art, but 10-20 per cent Grand Cru would be in the right area. Sour Grand Cru is available in Britain in bottle. Devotees can either obtain the sour beer by buying the genuine stuff and adding this at about 2.5 litres (4 pints) per 23 litre batch, priming and then maturing for a further 6 weeks, or they can attempt to make their own. See the Grand Cru recipe on the next page and the article on sour beers in the appendices.

RODENBACH
GRAND CRU

Belgian sour ale. An assertively sour beer used mainly for blending purposes to produce the beer called, simply, "Rodenbach" (see previous recipe), which is similar to old-time London Porter. Grand Cru is sold as a beer in its own right, but it is so sour that even local Belgian drinkers often add a splash of grenadine or cherry juice to make it more palatable.

ORIGINAL GRAVITY   1064   15.8° Plato

	25 litres	23 litres	5 UK gals	5 US gals
Pale malt	4,950 gm	4,550 gm	9.85 lb	8.2 lb
Flaked maize	1,450 gm	1,300 gm	2.85 lb	2.35 lb
Caramunich malt	700 gm	670 gm	1.4 lb	1.2 lb
Chocolate malt	100 gm	90 gm	3.2 oz	2.7 oz

START OF BOIL

	25 litres	23 litres	5 UK gals	5 US gals
Golding hops	35 gm	30 gm	1.1 oz	.9 oz

BREWING METHOD
Temperature-stepped infusion or double-decoction mash. Top-fermenting yeast

MASH SCHEDULE	52°C - 20 minutes	
	62°C - 40 minutes	
	72°C - 40 minutes	
BOIL TIME	90 minutes	
RACKING GRAVITY	1016	3.9° Plato
ALCOHOL CONTENT	6.6% by volume	5.1% by weight
BITTERNESS	14 EBU	
COLOUR	60 EBC	

The commercial version of this beer is deliberately soured by ageing it for eighteen months to two years or more in unlined oak vats, in the same way old-time London porters used to be. During this ageing period a microbiological cocktail of several micro-organisms work on the beer, acidifying it in the process. Various varieties of acetic acid bacteria, lactic acid bacteria and brettanomyces "wild" yeast produce various different acids; lactic, acetic, and citric probably being the most dominant. Oak vats or casks are used because the wood is semi-pervious to air and some of the micro-organisms are aerobic. The difficulty for amateur production is to duplicate this slight permeability. See article on soured beers in the appendices and the previous recipe (Rodenbach).

SCHLENKERLA
RAUCHBIER

Bamberg dark smoked beer. Intense smoked malt aroma and palate, big finish dominated by smoked malt and dark grain with a delicate hint of chocolate.

ORIGINAL GRAVITY	1054	13.3° Plato

	25 litres	23 litres	5 UK gals	5 US gals
Rauchmalt malt	6,010 gm	5,530 gm	12.0 lb	10.0 lb
Chocolate malt	105 gm	96 gm	3.4 oz	2.8 oz

START OF BOIL

Hallertau hops	52 gm	48 gm	1.7 oz	1.4 oz

LAST 15 MINUTES OF BOIL

Irish moss	10 gm	10 gm	.35 oz	.30 oz

BREWING METHOD
Temperature-stepped infusion or double-decoction mash. Top-fermenting yeast

MASH SCHEDULE	50°C - 20 minutes (122°F)
	65°C - 60 minutes (149°F)
	76°C - 10 minutes (169°F) then run off
BOIL TIME	90 minutes
RACKING GRAVITY	1013 3.1° Plato
ALCOHOL CONTENT	5.5% by volume 4.4% by weight
BITTERNESS	30 EBU
COLOUR	52 EBC

This is a classic Bamberger smoked beer using beech-smoked malt. The genuine stuff, imported from Germany, is available from many home-brew shops. Every home brewer should try a smoked beer at least once. The brewery claim to use a double decoction mash, but a temperature stepped mash is the modern equivalent. The 76°C stage can be omitted if desired, it is not really necessary in the home brew environment. The beer is conditioned for four to six months.

SCHNEIDER
AVENTINUS

Bavarian weizen doppelbock. Rich, dark sultana fruit aroma, dark fruit and spices in the mouth, long, complex finish with dark malt, fruit and gentle hops.

ORIGINAL GRAVITY 1077   18.5° Plato

	25 litres	23 litres	5 UK gals	5 US gals
Wheat malt	5,360 gm	4,930 gm	10.7 lb	8.9 lb
Munich malt	1,340 gm	1,240 gm	2.65 lb	2.2 lb
Lager malt (Pilsen)	1,260 gm	1,160 gm	2.5 lb	2.1 lb
Caramunich malt	970 gm	890 gm	1.9 lb	1.6 lb

START OF BOIL

Hallertau hops	40 gm	35 gm	1.2 oz	1.0 oz

LAST 15 MINUTES OF BOIL

Hallertau hops	10 gm	10 gm	.35 oz	.30 oz
Irish moss	10 gm	10 gm	.35 oz	.30 oz

BREWING METHOD
Temperature-stepped infusion or double-decoction mash. Top-fermenting yeast

MASH SCHEDULE	50°C - 20 minutes (122°F)
	65°C - 60 minutes (149°F)
	76°C - 10 minutes (169°F) then run off
BOIL TIME	90 minutes
RACKING GRAVITY	1019 4.2° Plato
ALCOHOL CONTENT	7.8% by volume 6.1% by weight
BITTERNESS	22 EBU
COLOUR	43 EBC

The brewery uses a double decoction mash, but the temperature stepped mash is perfectly satisfactory. The 76°C stage can be omitted.

SCHNEIDER
WEISSE

Bavarian wheat beer. The classic Bavarian wheat beer with a tart apple fruit aroma, quenching fruit in the mouth, big finish with apple, banana and bubblegum.

ORIGINAL GRAVITY   1054   13.3° Plato

	25 litres	23 litres	5 UK gals	5 US gals
Wheat malt	3,770 gm	3,470 gm	7.5 lb	6.25 lb
Lager malt (pilsner)	1,060 gm	980 gm	2.1 lb	1.75 lb
Vienna malt	1,070 gm	980 gm	2.1 lb	1.75 lb
Caramunich malt	360 gm	330 gm	11.3 oz	9.4 oz

START OF BOIL

Hallertau hops	25 gm	20 gm	.7 oz	.6 oz

LAST 15 MINUTES OF BOIL

Hallertau hops	10 gm	10 gm	.35 oz	.30 oz
Irish moss	10 gm	10 gm	.35 oz	.30 oz

BREWING METHOD
Temperature-stepped infusion or double-decoction mash. Top-fermenting yeast

MASH SCHEDULE	50°C - 20 minutes (122°F)	
	65°C - 60 minutes (149°F)	
	76°C - 10 minutes (169°F) then run off	
BOIL TIME	90 minutes	
RACKING GRAVITY	1012	3.0° Plato
ALCOHOL CONTENT	5.6% by volume	4.5% by weight
BITTERNESS	13 EBU	
COLOUR	19 EBC	

The 76°C mashing stage is unnecessary in the home brewing environment and can be omitted. The simple two-temperature stepped mash is perfectly adequate. Ferment as an ale at 18-22°C (50-59°F).

SIGL WEIZEN
GOLD

Austrian wheat beer. Fresh and inviting hop and cloves aroma. Refreshing in the mouth, gentle, lingering bitter-sweet finish. A quenching and fruity wheat beer produced by a small independent family firm which claims to be the only one in Austria to adhere to the German Purity Pledge.

ORIGINAL GRAVITY	1050	12.3° Plato

	25 litres	23 litres	5 UK gals	5 US gals
Pale malt	3,680 gm	3,380 gm	7.35 lb	6.1 lb
Wheat malt	1,980 gm	1,820 gm	3.95 lb	3.3 lb

START OF BOIL

	25 litres	23 litres	5 UK gals	5 US gals
Hallertau hops	35 gm	30 gm	1.1 oz	.9 oz

LAST 15 MINUTES OF BOIL

	25 litres	23 litres	5 UK gals	5 US gals
Hallertau hops	10 gm	10 gm	.35 oz	.30 oz
Irish moss	10 gm	10 gm	.35 oz	.30 oz

BREWING METHOD
Single-infusion mash; top-fermenting yeast

MASH SCHEDULE	66°C - 90 minutes	
BOIL TIME	90 minutes	
RACKING GRAVITY	1011	2.8° Plato
ALCOHOL CONTENT	5.2% by volume	4.2% by weight
BITTERNESS	20 EBU	
COLOUR	9 EBC	

Appendix 1: Soured beers

A number of European beers are intentionally sour. Most of these examples are of Belgian origin, but Germany produces a few and Guinness Foreign Extra Stout is also a soured beer. The sourness ranges from overpoweringly sour, such as Lambic or Rodenbach Grand Cru; moderately sour, such as gueuze or blended Rodenbach; slightly sour, like some wheat beers and whites; and those that have a background sourness that is barely perceptible, but nevertheless, acts as a superb flavour enhancer that accentuates the maltiness. Guinness Foreign Extra Stout is in this class.

The techniques used to make most of these beers stem from traditions going back hundreds of years. I suspect that prior to the pale ale revolution most beers that were matured for any length of time were sour, because not only was there very little that old-time brewers could do about it with the weaker beers, but a background sourness was highly esteemed by many drinkers. Old-time porter was a soured beer, although I know of no modern examples of porter that are.

Various kinds of souring technique still exist today. The classic traditional form of souring, such as that of old-time porter, modern Rodenbach, or Lambic occurs during lengthy maturation periods by the action of certain micro-organisms that most beer-writers refer to euphemistically as "wild yeasts". Two other souring methods, both used by some German brewers, include inoculating the beer or the mash with certain lactobacillus strains. Also, some strains of commercial brewing yeast impart a slightly sour character to a beer.

SOURING DURING MATURATION

The classic form of souring, certainly prevalent in Europe, including Britain, up to the late 1800s, took place during maturation by what brewers of the time referred to as secondary fermentation. Nowadays, certainly in home brewing, we understand secondary fermentation to mean the generation of conditioning gas in cask or bottle within a few days or weeks of filling, as an ongoing process of primary fermentation. However, in old-time brewing it did not mean the same thing: secondary fermentation literally meant a secondary fermentation caused by secondary (wild) yeasts such as Brettanomyces strains. These secondary fermentations occurred spontaneously as violent "frets" in the cask while the beer was being matured in the brewer's cellar, sometimes several months into maturation, and the brewer had to vent the casks until the frets were over. Although the brewers of the time were probably unaware that wild yeasts were responsible for these frets, they did realise from experience that the beers did not sour until these frets had occurred.

Many commercial brewing books, even relatively modern ones, contain passages that hark back to the days when these secondary fermentations were important. Consider this taken from Brewing – Theory and Practice, 1956 edition.

"The secondary fermentation will develop spontaneously. As soon as it is noted a porous peg should be inserted in the cask in order to ease the pressure of gas. Immediately the pressure has slackened a hard peg must be substituted or the beer may flatten to a degree from which it might never recover. Generally one fret in the brewery cellar is sufficient for ordinary beer, but for extra strong ales which are stored for many months, two or even three frets in the cask may be necessary. If any difficulty is experienced in bringing them into action, a vigorous rolling coupled with a slight rise in cellar temperature will generally have the desired effect."

That passage is taken from the 1956 edition of the aforementioned book. The first edition was published in 1936, but it is certainly based on a much earlier work than even that; the deliberate souring of beers in Britain was just about extinct by the late 19th century.

In contrast, James Herbert in Practical Brewing, 1871, stated that secondary fermentations are bad for the beer and should be avoided at all costs, although he does not give any practical advice for avoiding them. There is a considerable amount of discrepancy and contradiction regarding the subject of secondary fermentations and sourness in contemporary brewing books, but this, I suspect, reflects regional preferences as to whether or not soured beer was relished from a local point of view.

Nevertheless, with this type of beer the souring took place in oak casks or large oak vats during maturation. The use of oak is important because oak has a slight porosity to air, and the souring micro-organisms that are active in this instance are mostly aerobic. Also, the wood interior of the cask or vat provides seed sites for aerobic bacteria to form and the small amount of air diffusing through the wood enables them to work slowly without interfering with other processes. With all the soured beers of this type that survive today, including Guinness, Rodenbach and the Lambics, the maturation still takes place in oak.

To understand why so called wild yeasts remain dormant during primary fermentation and then rise up many weeks into maturation we need to touch on a subject not much talked about in home brewing circles nor very widely understood. That of oxidation potential.

OXIDATION-REDUCTION OR REDOX
POTENTIAL (RH)

Oxidation and reduction are fundamental processes in all living things. Respiration of man and animals is an oxidative process and so is fermentation. Sometimes free oxygen is involved, such as when we breathe or when yeast is respiring aerobically during its growth phase, but more often oxidation is performed by one molecule giving up oxygen to another. Fermentation, for instance, is caused by sugar giving up oxygen to an oxidative enzyme secreted by the yeast. Alcohol and carbon dioxide are what remains when a sugar molecule is deprived of an oxygen atom. For every oxidative process of this sort there must also be a corresponding reduction process. In the fermentation example, when the sugar gives up its oxygen atom the enzyme has been oxidised, but the sugar has been reduced. The situation is complicated because you do not actually need oxygen to oxidise something, you can perform the same function by removing hydrogen or by removing electrons.

To oversimplify a somewhat complicated concept, the oxidation-reduction potential of a beer is the likelihood of a micro-organism or any other chemical reaction getting enough oxygen to satisfy its needs, or the likelihood of reduction taking place by some other mechanism. In home brewing we can view it simply as being the potential oxygen available.

Oxidation-reduction potential is often termed Redox potential. Like pH, it is measured in terms of hydrogen ions and is given the symbol rH. pH meters can usually also measure rH by attaching an rH probe. rH is important because various micro-organisms can only exist or function within certain rH limits in the same way that they can only exist or grow within certain pH limits. Because both pH and rH are measured in terms of hydrogen, a change in pH will usually bring about a corresponding change in rH.

During primary fermentation the primary yeast rapidly establishes conditions that favour itself and that are alien to other micro-organisms. When the yeast is first pitched the pH of the beer falls rapidly from about pH 5.3 to a value of about pH 4; and the rH falls from a very high value to the low value of about rH 10. Under these conditions wild yeasts and most other micro-organisms cannot thrive, although any that are present are not necessarily killed; they just remain dormant until conditions are correct for them.

When the beer is put into oak casks or large oak vats, the primary yeast is still fairly active, working on residual sugars and dextrins. The rH is maintained at about 10 because any oxygen that comes along is immediately scavenged by the primary yeast. Eventually, however, the beer runs out of essential nutrients, amino-acids and the like, and the sugar balance is wrong to support the primary yeast. The primary yeast begins to go dormant, or go into tick-over mode, and cells begin to die off.

With the primary yeast dormant the rH begins to rise, either by gradual diffusion of air through the walls of the oak maturation vessel or by other chemical processes. The dead cells autolyse (get consumed by their own enzyme system) and in so doing release their nutrients back into the beer. When the rH has risen above about rH 15 and sufficient nutrients have been returned to the beer, and pH and temperature conditions are satisfied, wild yeasts and other micro-organisms can then become active and they rise up and acidify the beer.

Of the various micro-organisms responsible for the souring, each one can become active in turn as conditions become suitable for it. Eventually, conditions become correct for the primary yeast to become dominant again, and things tick along as normal until the next uprising of wild yeast, and the cycle may repeat itself several times over a period of many months.

OLD-TIME PORTER, RODENBACH AND
SOURED ALES

Although there are no old-time porter recipes in this book, Rodenbach is certainly the modern commercial beer that is nearest to what old time porter must have been like. Indeed, it seems likely that Rodenbach may have had its origins in the porter tradition. The Belgian Rodenbach brewery was founded in 1820, during porter's heyday, and it is known that members of the Rodenbach family studied brewing in London. The only difference between the making of modern Rodenbach and old-time porter of the early 1800s, is that old-time porter used smoked brown malt, as I suspect that Rodenbach did too during the 19th century.

Old-time porter, Rodenbach, Guinness Foreign Extra Stout, and some Belgian soured ales are a blend of two beers; a beer that has been aged for a long time and is very sour, and a fresh beer that is not sour. This blending technique enables beers to be produced with the right degree of sourness, and is a very economical way of making soured beers because only a fraction of the brewer's output needs to be matured for any length of time – the vast majority of the blend is fresh, almost immature beer.

Rodenbach is a blend of a strong, sour beer of OG about 1065 that has been aged for 18 months to 2 years, and a weaker, fresher, unsour beer of OG about 1047 that has been aged for only four or five weeks. The hop rates are deliberately kept low so as not to inhibit the souring micro-organisms. The blending ratio is probably 10-20 per cent sour to 80-90 per cent fresh, depending on the final acidity of the sour beer. The sour beer is sold separately under the name Grand Cru and it is important not to mistake the confusingly named and moderately sour Rodenbach for the assertively sour Rodenbach Grand Cru. Those brewers who want to make an emulation of standard Rodenbach can buy bottled Grand Cru as the souring agent and add this to their home brewed beer in about a 10 per cent ratio, increasing the dose further if the sourness is not assertive enough.

Making a Grand Cru oneself, however, will be considerably more difficult. The main souring micro-organisms are various Brettanomyces species of wild yeast, Dekkera species (sexual state of Brettanomyces), certain acetic and lactic bacteria, and several more. According to Michael Jackson about 20 micro-organisms are responsible for the souring of Rodenbach. Getting hold of the micro-organisms is relatively easy; they are around us in the air and are abundant on barley and malt.

A major problem would be imitating the slight porosity of oak in the absence of oak casks. This slight porosity, I suspect, aids in raising the redox potential of the beer over a period of time, allowing successively different microbes to come into play. More importantly, it seems likely that highly aerobic acetic acid bacteria seed themselves in the oak and acetify the beer from the wood surface. It must be significant that all the producers of this type of soured beer perform the souring function in wood. Under these conditions the aerobic micro-organisms work very slowly which is why it takes eighteen months to two years for this souring to take place. Another problem would be acquiring the patience to wait eighteen months or more.

To make a Grand Cru ferment the beer in the conventional sense using a highly attenuative ale yeast, or a mixture of several strains. Rodenbach beers are pasteurised so their multi-strain primary yeast cannot be lifted from it, but yeast can be cultured from some Liefman's beers and their yeast is said to have originated at Rodenbach. Nevertheless, any good, highly attenuative real ale yeast would do fine.

After fermentation is complete, cask the beer and leave the cask at normal fermentation temperature for three to four weeks. When the three weeks has elapsed, open the cask and add a handful of raw barley malt. Alternatively, or in addition, draw off half a pint of the beer into a broad glass and leave in the open air for 24 hours, preferably outdoors in a sheltered rain-proof position but not in high summer. Add this to the cask, reseal and leave for twelve months. Brettanomyces cultures are available from some sources, and these can be added as insurance if available. Once you have successfully made a soured beer, you can keep a bottle of it back to re-seed your next batch.

LAMBICS

Lambics are soured during long maturation periods by 70-80 different micro-organisms. Lambic beers have rather more access to air during maturation than beers like Rodenbach, and the almost non-existent hop rate allows more organisms to survive.

Some Lambics rely entirely on wild microbes to perform the fermentation and have no conventional fermentation stage. After mashing and boiling, the beer is run into shallow cooling trays in the brewery attic, behind slatted wooden louvres to the outside world, where the beer cools and also picks up its micro-organisms from the air. After this the beer is run directly into the casks, and fermentation is conducted in cask.

Other Lambic producers pick up micro-organisms in the cooling tray in the conventional manner, but add a top-working ale yeast for the primary fermentation stage. In some cases the beer is run into conventional fermentation vessels, but is only there for a day or two, and the beer is run into the casks before fermentation is complete.

The unique thing about Lambics is that primary and secondary fermentation is usually conducted in cask and the cask is never tightly sealed; the beer is allowed to go flat. When the beer is first run from the coolers into the cask, the bunghole is left open and surplus yeast from primary fermentation is allowed to escape through the bunghole. When yeast stops issuing from the bunghole, a muslin-type cloth is sometimes placed over the bunghole to keep creepy crawlies out, but the cask is still vented to the atmosphere. When fermentation has abated, and the beer is quiet, a wedge surrounded by cloth is forced into the bunghole, which effectively seals the cask, but not gas-tight. Any carbon dioxide generated by secondary fermentation can escape and air can diffuse in.

The beer goes flat during maturation, so any micro-organism that has a carbon dioxide requirement is inhibited, and those microbes that are inhibited by carbon dioxide are permitted to thrive. Various Brettanomyces strains thrive, Candida species, various lactic and acetic acid bacteria and about 70 more. Aerobic surface film yeasts and oxidative sherry-type flora are also present.

To make this type of beer, I would add a top-working yeast strain for primary fermentation in the normal home-brew manner. To acquire the souring microbes, a glass of the sweet wort prior to fermentation or a glass of beer after primary fermentation can be left in the open air for twenty-four hours to pick up micro-organisms in the traditional Lambic fashion. A handful of raw barley and raw wheat can be thrown into the cask for good measure, or a fair old cocktail of microbes can be cultured up from unpasteurised Lambic on sale.

It is often said that the Lambic character can only be acquired by capturing micro-organisms from the Lambic region, but I doubt it. If you compare half a dozen commercial Lambics side by side, they all taste completely different even though the breweries are all situated within a couple of miles of each other. It is true that if the commercial brewery is situated close to orchards or cereal growing areas the airborne microflora will be in a different balance to that in, say,

Watford, but samples of all the species will usually be present. Wind knows no national barriers.

The beers can be casked in conventional home-brew casks, but with the cap only lightly screwed down so that the seal is not gas tight. I suppose all that remains is to put it to one side and wait for two or three years. Whereas Lambics are usually flat and lifeless, Gueuze is a blend of old and young Lambics, primed and re-yeasted to induce carbonation. The proportion of young beer is usually between 50-70 per cent depending upon taste and the degree of sourness required. Some types of Gueuze are a blend of Lambic and a conventional beer.

SOUR MASH BEERS

Some German breweries encourage lactic acid bacteria, Lactobacillus delbrueckii, to grow in the mash to acidify the beer, lower the pH, and provide a lactic character. The source of the L. delbrueckii is our good old favourite: raw barley malt. All barley malt is teeming with the stuff, generally picked up during storage in the maltster's garners. Selectivity is provided due to the fact that L. delbrueckii is thermophilic, will thrive comfortably at temperatures of 50°C (122°F) or more, whereas competing bacteria will be killed or inhibited by prolonged exposure to those temperatures.

Lactobacillus delbrueckii has a glucose requirement, so some saccharification of the mash must take place before the bacteria can get to work. Fortunately, slow saccharification takes place at 50°C, so it is only necessary to carefully adjust the temperature of the mash to 50°C (122°F), without exceeding that temperature by much, and leave for 24-48 hours or until the pH has dropped to about pH 3.5-4. you can stir in a couple of handfuls of raw, uncrushed malt for insurance, but it usually is not necessary (The heat generated when crushing the malt can be enough to destroy the bacteria). The mash is then raised to saccharification temperature and the mash performed in the normal way.

Some brewers begin the mash at 65°C (149°F) for twenty minutes or so to ensure sufficient substrate exists for the bacteria to work on, then cool the mash to 50°C (122°F), stir in a couple of handfuls of raw malt, and then leave for 24-48 hours or until the pH has dropped to 3.5-4. The temperature is then raised to normal saccharification temperatures and the mash completed. Unfortunately, this method can destroy the protein-rest enzymes, should a rest be required.

A popular home-brew method is to sour only a proportion of the mash about two days before the main mash is due to begin. A mini-mash consisting of about 10-15 per cent of the main mash is made up, mashed at 65°C (149°F) for one hour, cooled to 50°C (122°F), a handful of raw malt stirred in, and the mini-mash left for 48 hours to acidify. When the main mash is made up, it is started at 50°C, the mini-mash stirred in, the mash readjusted to 50°C, and mashing performed

177

in the normal way, standing the mash for half an hour or more at 50°C before raising to normal saccharification temperatures. This has the benefit of preserving the important enzymes.

It is important that the souring part of the mash or the mini-mash is maintained at 50°C for as long as possible during the 24-48 hour standing period. This favours Lactobacillus delbrueckii, but is alien to other forms of bacteria. The mash tun should be very well insulated, but the temperature will inevitably drop during such a long standing period. The mash can be returned to 50°C from time to time if at all possible, but it probably is not necessary.

A surprising number of moulds and fungi can grow on the surface of the mash during a 48 hours stand. They are harmless, but they usually put people off a bit. These moulds are aerobic and need air, whereas L. delbrueckii is anaerobic and does not. The moulds can be inhibited by tightly covering the surface of the mash with polythene to keep air out. Bubble wrap is the best stuff to use for this purpose because it will greatly enhance the insulation properties of the mash, maintaining the crucial 50°C for longer. Use several layers and press it well down on to the surface of the mash. A small amount of mould will escape the defences and form, but this can be scraped off when the souring is complete.

LACTOBACILLUS INOCULATION

A number of beers, particularly German Berliner-style wheat beers are inoculated with lactic acid bacteria in the fermenter. Again the preferred microbe is Lactobacillus delbrueckii, and it is obtained in a similar way to the previous method. In this case, make up a micro-mash using crushed pale malt at 65-66°C in a domestic vacuum-flask and stand for one-and-a-half hours. Cool, or allow to cool naturally, to 50°C (122°F), mix in a quantity of uncrushed malt, fit the cap and stand for 24-48 hours.

Alternatively, make up a malt extract solution of about OG 1040-50, boil for fifteen minutes, cool to 60°C (140°F) and add to the vacuum-flask, when the solution has cooled to 50°C, add a quantity of uncrushed malt, fit the cap and stand for 24-48 hours.

In both cases the culture is used by straining the fluid from the grains and adding to the fermenter. L. delbrueckii has a glucose requirement, and the bacteria is unlikely to compete well in the presence of active brewers yeast. In the case of Berliner wheat beers it is usual to add the bacteria culture a few hours before the yeast to give the bacteria a head start. In some instances the yeast and bacteria are added together.

WATER TREATMENT FOR SOURED BEERS

Notwithstanding my comments regarding water treatment elsewhere in this book, it is often stated in home brewing books that dark beers prefer carbonate water and pale beers prefer gypseous water. This I believe to be a load of old bunkum, but it may be true to say that soured beers prefer carbonate water and unsoured beers prefer gypseous water. The fact that dark beers were usually soured beers, like London stout and porter; and pale beers were usually unsoured, like the pale ales of Burton, may be the historical reason for this widely held misconception. These long-term, widely held beliefs must represent centuries of accumulated wisdom of some sort, and I have always been intrigued as to the origin of this, because we can't allow accumulated wisdom go to waste. A century ago the statement would have been quite true, but few brewers make soured beers any more, and that's what threw the spanner in the works.

The fact is that gypsum does inhibit a number of micro-organisms, particularly yeasts, and the lower pH that gypsum induces in the beer will inhibit a number of bacteria. It is possible to force brewer's yeast to sporulate by subjecting it to high levels of gypsum, indicating that the yeast is in some sort of stress, although it seems to be able to cope comfortably with levels normally used in brewing. However, the same may not be said of Brettanomyces strains; relatively low levels of gypsum may inhibit the development of these yeasts.

Historically, London brewers were unable to make decent pale ales and the brewers of Burton upon Trent were unable to make decent porter. It may have been that the London brewers were unable to prevent their pale ales from souring and the Burton brewers were unable to sour their porters satisfactorily. My current theory is that the pale ales of Burton upon Trent reigned supreme in India because Brettanomyces strains of yeast were suppressed by the gypsum and did not often rise up during the long journey to India and cause burst casks and other maladies in the ship. Burton beers were certainly very stable, and gypsum must have been the reason.

With these theories in mind, and I stress that they are only theories, I would be inclined not to treat water used for soured beers of the old-time porter or Rodenbach style. If limited water treatment is performed, I would suggest not adding gypsum. I doubt if carbonate levels are particularly significant, so it probably does not matter if the water is boiled or not, but we might as well give accumulated wisdom the benefit of the doubt.

BLENDED, VATTED ALES

There are certain types of unsoured ale that are stored for long periods and then blended with a weaker beer. These are known in commercial brewerspeak as vatted ales. A strong beer is matured for a long period and during this time it picks up certain maturation characteristics, esters, fruitiness, and nutty characteristics that would not be formed if a weaker beer was matured for a long period. This strong, mature beer is then blended, in relatively small quantities, with a weak, less mature beer. The combination produces a moderately weak beer, say OG 1040, displaying flavour characteristics typical of a much stronger beer. A number of brewers practise this technique: Liefmans beers, certain Greene King beers, Newcastle Brown, and a number of the weaker, so called, old ales are made this way.

This technique began way back in time as method of being able to supply some beer in the summer in the days when sound ale could not be brewed during the summer months due to problems with infection. Normally brewers had to brew all their beer during the winter and shut down for the summer months. A very strong, winter-brewed ale was matured for six months or a year and then blended with fresh summer-brewed beer. The combination produced a palatable summer beer that could be sent out of the brewery immediately, and was consumed before it had a chance to go off. The technique was called "bringing forward" in old-time brewerspeak and was practised by Brakspears of Henley by 1800 and doubtless by other brewers long before that. In these modern times of weaker, non-matured, running beers it is a useful method of producing a beer of greater character than the norm.

Appendix 2: Conversion tables

Correction table for 20°C hydrometers

Temperature (°C)	Correction
4-5	−2.0
5-12	−1.5
12-16	−1.0
16-19	−0.5
19-21	0
21-23	+0.5
23-24	+1.0
24-27	+1.5
27-29	+2.0
29-31	+2.5
31-32	+3.0
32-34	+3.5
34-36	+4.0
36-38	+5.0
39-41	+6.0

Correction table for 60°C hydrometers

Temperature (°C)	Correction
34-49	−1.0
49-57	−0.5
57-63	0
63-68	+0.5
68-72	+1.0
72-76	+1.5
76-79	+2.0
79-82	+2.5
82-85	+3.0
85-88	+3.5
88-91	+4.0
91-94	+4.5
94-98	+5.0
98-102	+6.0
102-107	+7.0

Using the table
At a given wort temperature the correction is simply added to or subtracted from the indicated gravity reading as appropriate.

Example
If a sample of wort has a temperature of 28°C and an indicated gravity of 1042 using a 20°C hydrometer;

181

From the table, the correction factor at 28°C = +2.
Therefore true gravity = 1042 +2 = 1044

A domestic teaspoon holds approximately: 5 ml.
A domestic dessert spoon holds approximately: 10 ml.
A domestic tablespoon holds approximately: 15 ml.
A large coffee mug holds approximately: 300 ml.

1 cubic metre	= 33.315 cu ft.
	= 219.98 Imperial gallons
	= 264.18 U.S. gallons
	= 1000 litres
	= 10hl
1 cubic foot	= 6.25 Imperial gallons
	= 5.2 U.S. gallons
1 Imp. gallon	= 4 quarts
	= 8 pints
	= 32 gills
	= 160 fluid ounces
	= 4.546 litres
	= 1.2 US gallons

To convert:

Ounces to grams	Multiply by: 28.35
Pounds to kilograms	Multiply by: 0.454
Imp. pints to litres	Multiply by: 0.568
Imp. gallons to litres	Multiply by: 4.546
U.K. to U.S. Gallons	Multiply by: 1.200
Lbs per barrel to S.G.	Multiply by: 2.778

To convert the other way, divide by the figure shown.

Imperial capacity conversions

25 litres	= 5.5 imp gallons	= 44 pints
5 litres	= 1.09 imp gallons	= 8 pints 16 fl. oz.
4 litres	= 0.88 imp gallons	= 7 pints
3 litres	= 0.66 imp gallons	= 5 pints 6 fl. oz.
2 litres	= 0.44 imp gallons	= 3 pints 10 fl. oz.
1 litre	= 0.22 imp gallons	= 1 pint 15 fl. oz

Weight conversions

Metric to Imperial		Imperial to metric	
10 kg	= 22 lb	10 lb	= 4.536 kg
5 kg	= 11 lb	5 lb	= 2.268 kg
4 kg	= 8 lb, 13 oz	4 lb	= 1.814 kg
3 kg	= 6 lb, 9¾ oz	3 lb	= 1.361 kg
2 kg	= 4 lb, 6½ oz	2 lb	= 907 g
1 kg	= 2 lb, 3¼ oz	1 lb	= 454 g
500 g	= 1 lb, 1½ oz	½ lb	= 227 g
250 g	= 8¾ oz	¼ lb	= 113 g
125 g	= 4½ oz	1 oz	= 28.4 g
100 g	= 3½ oz	½ oz	= 14.2 g
50 g	= 1¾ oz	¼ oz	= 7.1 g
25 g	= ¾ oz	⅛ oz	= 3.5 g

Decimal fractions of a pound to ounces

.10 lb	= 1.6 oz	.55 lb	= 8.8 oz
.15 lb	= 2.4 oz	.60 lb	= 9.6 oz
.20 lb	= 3.2 oz	.65 lb	= 10.4 oz
.25 lb	= 4.0 oz	.70 lb	= 11.2 oz
.30 lb	= 4.8 oz	.75 lb	= 12.0 oz
.35 lb	= 5.6 oz	.80 lb	= 12.8 oz
.40 lb	= 6.4 oz	.85 lb	= 13.6 oz
.45 lb	= 7.2 oz	.90 lb	= 14.4 oz
.50 lb	= 8.0 oz	.95 lb	= 15.2 oz

The recipes for 5 gallon volumes give the ingredients in pounds plus a decimal part of a pound; ie, 9.6 lb. The above table converts the decimal part of a pound to ounces.

US conversions

1 US gallon	= 4 quarts
	= 8 pints
	= 32 gills
	= 128 US fluid ounces
	= 3.785 litres
	= 0.832 UK gallons

To convert:

Ounces to grams	Multiply by: 28.35
Pounds to kilograms	Multiply by: 0.454
U.S. pints to litres	Multiply by: 0.473
U.S. gallons to litres	Multiply by: 3.785
U.K. to U.S. Gallons	Multiply by: 1.200

To convert the other way, divide by the figure given.

US capacity conversions

25 litres	= 6.6 US gallons	= 52 pints 13 fl. oz.
5 litres	= 1.32 US gallons	= 10 pints 9 fl. oz.
4 litres	= 1.05 US gallons	= pints 7 fl. oz.
3 litres	= 0.79 US gallons	= 6 pints 6 fl. oz.
2 litres	= 0.52 US gallons	= 4 pints 4 fl. oz.
1 litre	= 0.26 US gallons	= 2 pints 2 fl. oz.

Hop substitution tables

The hop substitution tables are a quick and easy way to substitute a different variety of bittering hop in any given recipe. To use, simply find the nearest figure to the quantity of hops specified in the recipe, and move up or down the column to find the equivalent quantity of substitute hops to use. EBUs or IBUs are given on the top line for a 23 litre (5 UK Galls) batch.

HOP SUBSTITUTION CHART 10 to 50 EBUs

BITTERNESS	10	12.5	15	17.5	20	22.5	25	27.5	30	32.5	35	37.5	40	42.5	45	47.5	50
FUGGLE	20g	26g	31g	36g	41g	46g	51g	56g	61g	66g	72g	77g	82g	87g	92g	97g	102g
GOLDING	17g	22g	26g	30g	35g	39g	43g	48g	52g	56g	61g	65g	69g	74g	78g	82g	87g
HALLERTAU	17g	21g	25g	29g	33g	38g	42g	46g	50g	54g	59g	63g	67g	71g	75g	79g	84g
SAAZ (Zatec)	17g	21g	25g	29g	33g	38g	42g	46g	50g	54g	59g	63g	67g	71g	75g	79g	84g
TETTNANG	18g	23g	28g	32g	37g	41g	46g	51g	55g	60g	64g	69g	74g	78g	83g	87g	92g
BRAMLING CROSS	15g	19g	23g	27g	31g	35g	38g	42g	46g	50g	54g	58g	61g	65g	69g	73g	77g
PROGRESS	15g	19g	22g	26g	30g	33g	37g	41g	45g	48g	52g	56g	59g	63g	67g	70g	74g
WHITBREAD G.V.	15g	18g	22g	26g	29g	33g	37g	40g	44g	47g	51g	55g	58g	62g	66g	69g	73g
STYRIAN GOLDING	14g	18g	21g	25g	28g	32g	35g	39g	42g	46g	50g	53g	57g	60g	64g	67g	71g
B. COLUMBIAN	13g	16g	20g	23g	26g	30g	33g	36g	39g	43g	46g	49g	53g	56g	59g	62g	66g
NORTH'N BREWER	12g	15g	18g	21g	24g	27g	30g	33g	36g	39g	42g	45g	48g	51g	54g	58g	61g
CHALLENGER	12g	15g	18g	21g	24g	27g	30g	33g	36g	39g	42g	45g	48g	51g	54g	57g	60g
BULLION	12g	15g	17g	20g	23g	26g	29g	32g	35g	38g	41g	44g	47g	49g	52g	55g	58g
NORTHDOWN	12g	14g	17g	20g	23g	26g	29g	32g	35g	37g	40g	43g	46g	49g	52g	55g	58g
ZENITH	10g	13g	15g	18g	20g	23g	26g	28g	31g	33g	36g	38g	41g	43g	46g	49g	51g
OMEGA	9g	12g	14g	17g	19g	21g	24g	26g	28g	31g	33g	36g	38g	40g	43g	45g	47g
YEOMAN	9g	11g	13g	15g	17g	20g	22g	24g	26g	28g	30g	33g	35g	37g	39g	41g	43g
TARGET	8g	10g	12g	14g	16g	18g	21g	23g	25g	27g	29g	31g	33g	35g	37g	39g	41g
LIBERTY USA	18g	23g	28g	32g	37g	41g	46g	51g	55g	60g	64g	69g	74g	78g	83g	87g	92g
MOUNT HOOD USA	17g	21g	25g	29g	33g	38g	42g	46g	50g	54g	59g	63g	67g	71g	75g	79g	84g
WILLIAMETTE USA	17g	21g	25g	29g	33g	38g	42g	46g	50g	54g	59g	63g	67g	71g	75g	79g	84g
CASCADE USA	15g	19g	23g	27g	31g	35g	38g	42g	46g	50g	54g	58g	61g	65g	69g	73g	77g
GALENA USA	9g	12g	14g	16g	18g	21g	23g	25g	28g	30g	32g	35g	37g	39g	41g	44g	46g

HOP SUBSTITUTION CHART 50 to 90 EBUs

BITTERNESS	50	52.5	55	57.5	60	62.5	65	67.5	70	72.5	75	77.5	80	82.5	85	87.5	90
FUGGLE	102g	107g	112g	118g	123g	128g	133g	138g	143g	148g	153g	158g	164g	169g	174g	179g	184g
GOLDING	87g	91g	95g	100g	104g	108g	113g	117g	122g	126g	130g	135g	139g	143g	148g	152g	156g
HALLERTAU	84g	88g	92g	96g	100g	105g	109g	113g	117g	121g	125g	130g	134g	138g	142g	146g	151g
SAAZ (Zatec)	84g	88g	92g	96g	100g	105g	109g	113g	117g	121g	125g	130g	134g	138g	142g	146g	151g
TETTNANG	92g	97g	101g	106g	110g	115g	120g	124g	129g	133g	138g	143g	147g	152g	156g	161g	166g
BRAMLING CROSS	77g	81g	84g	88g	92g	96g	100g	104g	107g	111g	115g	119g	123g	127g	130g	134g	138g
PROGRESS	74g	78g	82g	85g	89g	93g	96g	100g	104g	108g	111g	115g	119g	122g	126g	130g	134g
WHITBREAD G.V.	73g	77g	80g	84g	88g	91g	95g	99g	102g	106g	110g	113g	117g	120g	124g	128g	131g
STYRIAN GOLDING	71g	74g	78g	81g	85g	88g	92g	96g	99g	103g	106g	110g	113g	117g	120g	124g	127g
B. COLUMBIAN	66g	69g	72g	76g	79g	82g	85g	89g	92g	95g	99g	102g	105g	108g	112g	115g	118g
NORTH'N BREWER	61g	64g	67g	70g	73g	76g	79g	82g	85g	88g	91g	94g	97g	100g	103g	106g	109g
CHALLENGER	60g	63g	66g	69g	72g	75g	78g	81g	84g	87g	90g	93g	96g	99g	102g	105g	108g
BULLION	58g	61g	64g	67g	70g	73g	76g	79g	82g	84g	87g	90g	93g	96g	99g	102g	105g
NORTHDOWN	58g	60g	63g	66g	69g	72g	75g	78g	81g	83g	86g	89g	92g	95g	98g	101g	104g
ZENITH	51g	54g	56g	59g	61g	64g	66g	69g	72g	74g	77g	79g	82g	84g	87g	89g	92g
OMEGA	47g	50g	52g	55g	57g	59g	62g	64g	66g	69g	71g	74g	76g	78g	81g	83g	85g
YEOMAN	43g	46g	48g	50g	52g	54g	56g	59g	61g	63g	65g	67g	69g	72g	74g	76g	78g
TARGET	41g	43g	45g	47g	49g	51g	53g	55g	58g	60g	62g	64g	66g	68g	70g	72g	74g
LIBERTY USA	92g	97g	101g	106g	110g	115g	120g	124g	129g	133g	138g	143g	147g	152g	156g	161g	166g
MOUNT HOOD USA	84g	88g	92g	96g	100g	105g	109g	113g	117g	121g	125g	130g	134g	138g	142g	146g	151g
WILLIAMETTE USA	84g	88g	92g	96g	100g	105g	109g	113g	117g	121g	125g	130g	134g	138g	142g	146g	151g
CASCADE USA	77g	81g	84g	88g	92g	96g	100g	104g	107g	111g	115g	119g	123g	127g	130g	134g	138g
GALENA USA	46g	48g	51g	53g	55g	58g	60g	62g	64g	67g	69g	71g	74g	76g	78g	81g	83g

Beers index

All the recipes are designed primarily to be mashed from grain, and all the recipes in this book can be made that way. However, some of the recipes also have a malt extract version given, and these are indicated by a (*).

ALES, ALTS, TRAPPIST

Main index